Peters Ammunition

THE PETERS CARTRIDGE CO.

CINCINNATI
U. S. A.

REPRINTED BY
COMMONWEALTH BOOK COMPANY

Copyright © 2022 by Commonwealth Book Company

All rights reserved. No part of this book may be reproduced in any form or by any means without the prior written consent of the publisher, excepting brief quotes used in reviews. Printed in the United States of America.

ISBN: 978-1-948986-49-6

Honor

    Strength

        Quality

            Service

QUALITY AMMUNITION

The development of modern small arms ammunition is inseparably linked with the history of The Peters Cartridge Company. From the date of its founding in 1887 it has constantly and consistently sought better processes, better materials and perfected workmanship, and through the successful combination of the efforts in these directions, it has inevitably resulted in the (P) brand being unrivaled today in the ammunition World.

The early years of the Company's existence were marked by many vicissitudes, but the history of the business has been a record of constant growth and improvement, obstacles met and surmounted and triumphs achieved, so that today the Company is an acknowledged leader in the industry and its product regarded by the trade and the consuming public as the World's *Standard*.

During the Great World War The Peters Cartridge Company completed all contracts with foreign Governments who were later our Allies, and when the United States entered the mighty conflict all the resources, facilities and energy of the Company were turned over to our Government: and how well it served is fully evidenced by a certificate of "Distinguished Service" presented to this Company by the United States Government, signed by the Secretary of War.

With the signing of the Armistice, which brought to an end War operations, thoughts again turned toward domestic requirements and The Peters Cartridge Company not only resumed the manufacturing of goods for domestic consumption in a remarkably short time, but produced in quality a totally superior product to anything ever before placed in the hands of the shooting public.

The main plant of The Peters Cartridge Company consists of several massive, steel reinforced, fireproof buildings, constructed within the last nine years, which were specifically designed and laid out for the manufacture of highest quality small arms ammunition, with full consideration given to economical production of same.

WORKS OF THE PETERS
LOCATED AT KINGS MILLS, OHIO

The Peters Cartridge Company employs the highest type of workmen, most of whom are residents of the model village of Kings Mills, Ohio. Their happy and contented disposition is the result of the very pleasant home life enjoyed by all, made possible by the systematic manner in which the village is operated. Rents are cheap, with ample ground for home gardening. Inhabitants have unusual opportunities for recreation, including swimming and fishing in the picturesque Little Miami river, theatre, library, gun and rifle club, athletic sports, etc. In addition the village maintains a fine church. The big majority of these employees are enthusiastic shooters either in the field, at the traps, or on the range. Wherever producers are consumers it follows that more interest will be taken in the manufacture of that which is produced and that greater care will be exercised by each and every employee in the performance of his duties—for being entirely familiar with the consumer's requirements, he knows how very important it is that every operation in the making of a shell or cartridge be exactly as it should be to produce the desired results.

The education of the young folks is taken care of at a fine large school, both Elementary and High.

Such are the surroundings of those who work in the great factory of The Peters Cartridge Company. The high standard of home life enjoyed by each and every employee is bound to reflect itself in the work performed by these people. It is a well known axiom, that a good workman makes a good citizen, and vice-versa, and the fact that in the village there are no police of any kind indicates the high type of citizenry located

CARTRIDGE COMPANY
ABOUT TWENTY-FIVE MILES FROM CINCINNATI

there. The health of every employee is carefully guarded by a physician and trained nurses, in a modern and completely equipped hospital located at the factory. No employee can work for The Peters Cartridge Company who does not measure up to both mental and physical requirements.

The factory management in collaboration with the Purchasing Department provides for the various materials and the inspection and acceptance thereof. The materials for Peters metallic cartridges are copper and brass in sheets, from which the metallic shells are made; pig lead, tin, etc. for bullets; powder; and materials for priming mixtures. All bullets are made in accordance with Peters standards, in order to produce that best suited to the arm in which it is to be used. Many kinds of powders for the various cartridges manufactured are used but they must all measure up to established Peters requirements before they are accepted for loading. The powder suited to produce the best load is ascertained by scientific tests in the Ballistic Department. All ingredients that go to make up the different priming mixtures must be to Peters specifications.

Materials for loaded paper shot shells are sheet brass and sheet gilding for the shell heads and primers, shell paper, wad paper, powder, hair for the famous Peters "felt wadding", lead, antimony, etc. for the shot. All of these materials are provided especially for The Peters Cartridge Company under its own formulae and specifications, but nevertheless all materials that enter into Peters products, when received at the factory are subjected to the most rigid tests by the Peters laboratories before they are accepted for use and issued into process.

A section of the large and modernly equipped chemical laboratory of the Peters plant.

The laboratory is fully provided with the latest and most efficient testing equipment for performing both chemical analysis and physical tests. The most important operations of the laboratory are:

1. Analysis and inspection of all raw materials.

2. Collaboration with the Purchasing and Manufacturing Departments in the matter of drawing up specifications for each lot of raw materials, so that the best possible quality may be obtained.

3. Inspection and analysis of materials in process from each factory operation, on both metallic and shot gun cartridges.

4. Analysis and testing of finished goods in cooperation with the Ballistic Department.

The Research Department of the Laboratory is required to be constantly on the look-out for any chance to introduce improvements in the quality of goods. Much time is devoted to this end of the work and when an improvement is possible, no expense is spared and no unnecessary delay occasioned in adopting it.

Practically all important machines used in the production of Peters Ammunition were designed and built in our own Engineering Department.

CUPPING DEPARTMENT—Where the cups or shells for the various cartridges and shot shells are blanked from sheet metal. This is the first operation in the making of a shell or cartridge.

METALLIC CARTRIDGES

In dealing with metallic ammunition we have three main classifications, namely, Rim Fire, Center Fire Pistol and Revolver, Center Fire Military and Sporting cartridges.

In Metallic Cartridges, to fully and satisfactorily meet the demands of the trade a total of over 260 different sizes and styles of cartridges are manufactured, from the small .22 B. B. Cap to the large .45-90 cartridge.

RIM FIRE CARTRIDGES: Rim Fire shells are cupped from sheet gilding metal. (Gilding is an alloy of copper and zinc, high in copper, while brass is an alloy of zinc and copper containing less copper.) The cupping operation consists of blanking a disc and forming this into an open top cylinder or cup. After the cup is formed, it is annealed to soften the metal for the drawing operations. (A drawing operation is one in which the diameter of the piece and its side wall thickness are reduced and the metal thus displaced is carried into the length.)

The drawn shell is trimmed to length for the heading operation, which at the same time removes the uneven metal left after drawing.

Next comes the heading operation, which is the final mechanical operation before priming. The head of the shell, head thickness, size of primer cavity and final shell length are all controlled in this operation.

After washing thoroughly, the shells are delivered to the priming machines, where the mixture is placed in the cavity formed in the rim.

General view in the Metallic Department.

CENTER FIRE CARTRIDGES: Center Fire Shells consist of two main classes, reduced or "bottle necked" and straight. These are cupped from brass, trimmed and drawn in a manner similar to the Rim Fire shells. The heading operation is next, at which time the primer pocket is formed. After the straight shells are trimmed to the final length they are ready for the insertion of the primer.

The reduced or bottle necked shells, after heading, are annealed to soften the metal for the reducing or necking operation. This operation is controlled in the laboratory by microscopic examination of the structure of the metal. The reducing follows and is performed by a series of operations, bringing the neck of the shell to the proper shape and size. The shells are then trimmed to desired length and given a final neck anneal, an extremely important feature of the (P) line, which insures the proper temper to maintain the correct tension on the bullet and still not season crack. This is also controlled by the laboratory microscope.

Both classes of shells are now ready for the inserting of the primer, which operation is performed on presses especially designed for this purpose.

In the loading of Peters metallic cartridges, the correct charge of powder is deposited in the shell, the bullet inserted and then crimped into place. This is done on machines designed and built in our Engineering Department, which load accurate charges of powder, and which assure extreme accuracy, uniformity and velocity in every cartridge.

View in Ballistic Department, where the chronographs and other equipment for testing are installed. By means of the chronographs Peters Ammunition is being constantly tested for velocity and ignition time. Other equipment in this department tests for patterns, pressures, penetration, accuracy of bullets, etc.

Realizing the great importance to the shooter of having ammunition that never fails to do what is expected of it, even in the tightest pinch, The Peters Cartridge Company maintains at all times a very close check on all goods in process and all finished goods through constant testing and inspection. Peters Ballistic Department, under the direction of experts, has the latest and most modern equipment for conducting a full and complete test of every cartridge, from standpoint of ignition time, velocity, pressure, penetration, accuracy, primer testing, etc. This careful and constant checking to see that the finished goods at all times measure up to the high standard established by Peters makes possible ammunition which is absolutely dependable, and assures the user really superior results.

POWDERS LOADED
IN PETERS METALLIC CARTRIDGES

SEMI-SMOKELESS POWDER

Those of Peters metallic cartridges that are loaded with KING'S SEMI-SMOKELESS powder, give their users a far superior load to anything otherwise obtainable, in fact, there is no powder that can successfully compete with Semi-Smokeless for cleanliness, accuracy and uniformity. On the range, it has established records which will probably stand for years, and it has given users cleaner, more accurate and uniform ammunition than can be secured with any other powder.

Semi-Smokeless has the velocity of Smokeless powder, with the low breach pressure of black powder. It is neither black nor smokeless, nor a combination of the two, but is an entirely different product and a vastly superior one.

As stated, not only does Semi-Smokeless give extremely accurate and uniform results, but it is known for its cleanliness and lack of injury to the rifle barrel. No rifle or gun should be set aside for any length of time after using, without having the barrel properly cleaned and oiled, but hundreds of rounds of Semi-Smokeless ammunition can be fired thru a gun barrel, without causing fouling or interfering to any extent with the accuracy, and in no way injuring the barrel.

The Peters Cartridge Company is the exclusive user of Semi-Smokeless powder, and in cartridges where others load ordinary black powder, Peters supplies Semi-Smokeless, and therefore gives shooters of the brand superior ammunition at no increase in price. The statement is sometimes made with reference to other brands of ammunition that a powder is supplied which is just as good as Semi-Smokeless as loaded by Peters. *This* mere statement immediately standardizes Semi-Smokeless powder. It might be further stated that not one single grain of black powder is loaded behind a Peters bullet.

SMOKELESS POWDERS

Smokeless powders loaded in Peters metallic cartridges are standard American powders which we have found best adapted to give maximum life to the arm, combined with the highest velocity and ignition, consistent with pressures permissible in the various arms. We are absolutely free to, and do, take advantage of any improvement in powder, no matter by whom manufactured.

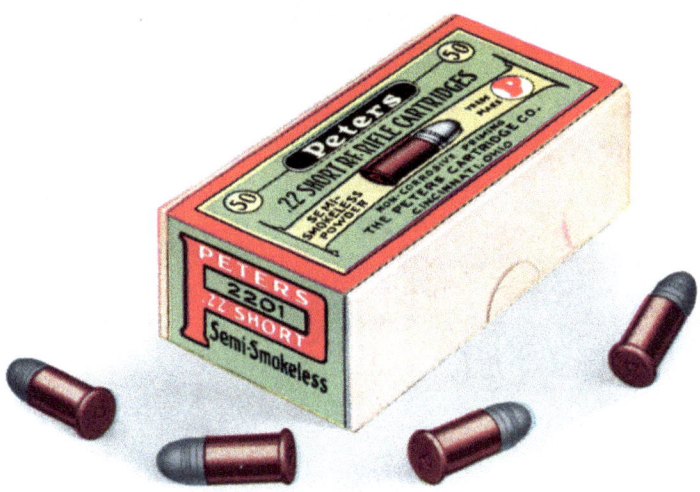

PETERS .22 SHORT CARTRIDGES

Semi-Smokeless   Smokeless

Especially adapted to Shooting Gallery use

We have given special attention toward producing a .22 Short Cartridge which would not only completely satisfy all commercial requirements including outdoor target practice, but which would give the greatest amount of satisfaction where used in shooting galleries. The gallery man requires a cartridge that is sure-fire, accurate, that will work perfectly in his rifles, and one that is clean shooting.

Peters .22 Short cartridges embody all of these important requisites to such a fine degree that it has been proven on more than one occasion that they are the most satisfactory gallery cartridges made. Galleries all over the country are coming more and more to 100% use of Peters cartridges. By producing a cartridge that fully meets every requirement of the shooting gallery it necessarily means that Peters "Shorts" are also superior for other uses. Remember, only in Peters cartridges, "Shorts" included, can the wonderful Semi-Smokeless powder be obtained. In all Peters Rim Fire cartridges the priming mixture is non-corrosive and non-erosive.

See page 18 for additional information.

PETERS .22 L. R. TACK-HOLE CARTRIDGES

Tack-Hole cartridges are specially made for the small bore shooter who desires unusually close, accurate grouping of his shots. Their extremely accurate and uniform shooting qualities have made them the favorite of many of the greatest marksmen in the World.

Every year in the small bore matches, users of "Tack-Hole" cartridges not only win many of the championships but in doing so, they establish records heretofore unheard of.

"Tack-Hole" ammunition scores exactly where the shooter holds. Not only is "Tack-Hole" remarkably accurate in its shooting, but it is also extremely clean shooting, and easy on the rifle barrel. Loaded with Semi-Smokeless powder, which has proven to be superior to powders used by others, in cleanliness, accuracy and uniformity, the shooter can fire his rifle hundreds of times without cleaning and still not interfere with the accuracy. Where a rifle is to be set aside for any length of time, it should be properly cleaned and oiled to avoid action of ordinary atmospheric conditions.

As in all Peters "Rim-Fire" cartridges, the priming mixture used in "Tack-Hole" ammunition is non-corrosive and non-erosive, so here again, users of the ⓟ brand have a distinct advantage.

(For further description and prices see page 20.)

PISTOL AND REVOLVER CARTRIDGES

The same great care and exacting requirements are insisted upon with regard to pistol and revolver sizes as in the case of all other Peters cartridges. In cartridges where other manufacturers load ordinary Black powder Peters supply the superior Semi-Smokeless powder.

In all sizes running from the small .22's to the .45's Peters Pistol and Revolver cartridges, whether Semi-Smokeless or Smokeless, assure their users of maximum results.

Police Departments all over the country are fast coming to the ⓟ Brand because of its proven dependability, accuracy and all around superiority.

In the United States Revolver Association matches, Peters pistol and revolver sizes always land the big share of the wins. "Where quality counts—they win".

HIGH VELOCITY
EXPANDING POINT

.25-20 WIN. and .32 WIN. (.32-20)
HIGH VELOCITY EXPANDING CARTRIDGES

For small, fast moving game these speedy cartridges with their improved expanding bullets are unequaled. Not only do they increase the range—lower the trajectory, but the uniform mushrooming qualities of the bullet combined with the high speed, results in a "whale of a punch", really surprising for a bullet of such weight. The .25-20 High Velocity Expanding cartridge is supplied with a 60 grain bullet and has a velocity of 2200 ft. per second with a muzzle energy of 645 ft. lbs., with trajectories at 100 yards 1.3 inches, 200 yards 8.2 inches, at mid-range.

The .32-20 High Velocity Expanding cartridge with a bullet weight of 80 grains has a muzzle velocity of 2000 ft. per second with a muzzle energy of 710 foot pounds, with trajectories of 1.4 inches for 100 yards and 7.6 inches for 200 yards at mid-range. With these ballistics and the superior type of expanding bullet, users are assured of maximum shocking power. See (pages 26 and 30.)

.25 REM. .25-35 AND .30-30
(HIGH VELOCITY)

Here again Peters maintains its leadership from the standpoint of improvements. Without reducing the bullet weight these popular cartridges have been speeded up, thus giving users of the (P) brand a distinct advantage from the standpoint of increased range, lower trajectory and greater shocking power, hence greater game-getting possibilities.

In cartridges designed for Big Game, if bullet weight is reduced to increase velocity, it follows that a certain amount of striking energy or shocking power will be sacrificed. In these Peters cartridges the standard bullet weights of 117 grs. for the .25 Rem. and .25-35, and 170 grs. for the .30-30 have been retained, although velocities have been increased, hence users are assured of really superior results, when compared with similar other cartridges on the market, where velocities have been increased at the sacrifice of bullet weight. In these Peters cartridges bullet weight is not reduced, although velocities have been increased.

(See pages 42, 43 and 86 for further information.)

ANOTHER PETERS DEVELOPMENT IN GAME CARTRIDGES

NEW TYPE EXPANDING BULLET WITH HIGHER VELOCITY AND INCREASED SHOCKING POWER

in .30-30 and .30 Rem.

Recent developments by The Peters Cartridge Company in the .30-30 and .30 Rem. cartridges provide a new improved type of expanding bullet (non-fouling), in two weights, driven at a velocity that is not only superior to similar other cartridges on the market, but which also makes possible greater all-around effectiveness for successful game-shooting.

These popular additions to the ⓟ line, because of their superior speed and new expanding bullet—which mushrooms perfectly on impact but which holds together well, insuring extreme penetration—increase the range, lower the trajectory, and develop terrific shocking power, the combination of which means greater chances of getting the game.

The new .30-30 cartridge—termed .30-30 M. C. Hollow Point Expanding, supplied in bullet weight of 125 grains, develops a velocity at the muzzle of 2,550 feet per second; muzzle energy 1,803 foot pounds.* Supplied in 165-grain bullet, muzzle velocity 2,250 f. s.; muzzle energy, 1,860 ft. lbs. The new .30 Rem. cartridge supplied with the improved M. C. Hollow Point Expanding bullet of 125-grain weight develops a muzzle velocity of 2,450 f. s.; muzzle energy, 1,665 ft. lbs. The 165-grain weight has a muzzle velocity of 2,250 f. s.; muzzle energy, 1,860 ft. lbs.

With the above new cartridges added to Peters regular .30-30 line with the standard bullet weights but having a velocity superior to similar other cartridges, the ⓟ line of the popular .30 caliber sizes is not only complete to answer any and every requirement but also superior from every standpoint of the shooter.

Actual Reproduction of Mushroomed Bullet

*See page 86 for complete ballistic information.

See pages 43 and 44 for list prices and other information.

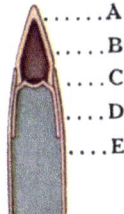
......A
.....B
....C
...D
....E

PROTECTED POINT EXPANDING BULLET
(Patented)

The demand of Big Game hunters for a bullet that combines penetration and mushrooming or expanding qualities, is fully met in Peters Protected Point Expanding Bullet (patented).

Note the cross-section view above. The tip (A) over the point prevents deformation in the magazine. On impact, the air in the chamber of the tip (B) is compressed, causing the instantaneous expansion of the jacket (C), which deforms the whole bullet, resulting in maximum shocking power. So that the bullet will retain its penetrating force, a cup (D) is placed over the end of the slug (E). This cup prevents the slug from breaking up.

As stated, the outstanding feature of the Protected Point Expanding Bullet is, that on impact it mushrooms perfectly, at the same time does not break up, consequently its penetrating powers are at a maximum. Most of the existing Big Game bullets do not deliver maximum shocking power, due to the fact that on impact, they frequently break up into pieces, and often in striking bone or hard tissue, do not have sufficient penetrating qualities to produce desired results. It has also been found in many cases that the ordinary Soft Nose bullet does not mushroom properly, especially when driven at the higher velocities.

We believe, that the Protected Point Expanding Bullet is the most effective Big Game bullet ever produced, and tests which we have conducted, and reports which we have received from experienced hunters, prove this bullet to be in a class by itself. Not only does the bullet develop maximum shocking power, but its remarkable accuracy assures longer, cleaner kills. As in the case of other Peters Military and Sporting bullets, the Protected Point Expanding type is constructed with Peters no-foul metal jacket.

As indicated on pages 42, 43, 44 and 45, we are supplying the Protected Point Expanding Bullet in the .30 Gov't '06, .30-40 Krag, .300 Savage, .270 Win., and .250-3000 Savage.

RIM FIRE CARTRIDGES

.22 B. B. CAP, ROUND BALL

Adapted to Flobert and all .22 calibre rim fire single shot rifles.

Smokeless powder, per 1,000	$ 3.50

Weight of bullet, 20 grains.
Packed 100 in a box, 10M in a case.

.22 C. B. CAP

Adapted to Flobert and all .22 caliber rim fire single shot rifles.

Semi-Smokeless powder, per 1,000	$ 4.40
Smokeless powder, lubricated, per 1,000	4.40
Smokeless powder, non-lubricated, per 1,000	4.40

Weight of bullet, 30 grains.
Packed 100 in a box, 10M in a case.

.22 SHORT   .22 SHORT HOLLOW POINT

Adapted to Winchester, Remington, Remington Auto Loading Mod. 24, and Colt Repeating rifles; Stevens, Remington and other single shot rifles; also pistols and revolvers of this caliber. Unequaled for shooting gallery use.

Semi-Smokeless powder, per 1,000	$ 5.00
Smokeless powder, lubricated, per 1,000	5.35
Smokeless powder, non-lubricated, per 1,000	5.35
Hollow Point, Semi-Smokeless powder, per 1,000	5.50
Hollow Point, Smokeless powder, lubricated, per 1,000	5.75
Hollow Point, Smokeless powder, non-lubricated, per 1,000	5.75

Weight of bullet, 30 grains.
Packed 50 in a box, 10M in a case.

Prices quoted in this catalogue are List Prices. Dealers supply Peters Ammunition at regular retail prices.

RIM FIRE CARTRIDGES

        .22 LONG   .22 LONG HOLLOW POINT

Adapted to Winchester, Remington, Colt and Marlin Repeating rifles; Stevens, Remington and other single shot rifles and pistols of this caliber.

Semi-Smokeless powder, per 1,000	$ 6.00
Smokeless powder, lubricated bullet, per 1,000	7.50
Smokeless powder, non-lubricated bullet, per 1,000	7.50
Hollow Point, Semi-Smokeless powder, per 1,000	6.50
Hollow Point, Smokeless powder, lubricated bullet, per 1,000	8.00
Hollow Point, Smokeless powder, non-lubricated, per 1,000	8.00

    Weight of bullet, 30 grains.
    Packed 50 in a box, 10M in a case.

      .22 LONG RIFLE   .22 LONG RIFLE HOLLOW POINT

Adapted to Marlin, Winchester, Remington Auto Loading Mod. 24, and Savage Repeating rifles; Remington, B. S. A., Savage, Stevens, Winchester, Iver-Johnson, and other single shot rifles; Colt, S. & W. and other revolvers; Colt Automatic, Reising, and other automatic pistols.

Smokeless powder, lubricated, per 1,000	$ 8.75
Smokeless powder, non-lubricated, per 1,000	8.75
Hollow Point, Smokeless, lubricated, per 1,000	9.35
Hollow Point, Smokeless, non-lubricated, per 1,000	9.35

    Weight of bullet, 40 grains; Hollow Point, 38 grains.
    Packed 50 in a box, 10M in a case.

   .22 LONG RIFLE (N. R. A.)   .22 LONG RIFLE (N. R. A.)
                                     HOLLOW POINT

Adapted to Winchester, Marlin, Remington Auto Loading Mod. 24, and Savage Repeating rifles; Remington, B. S. A., Savage, Stevens, Winchester, Iver-Johnson, and other single shot rifles; Colt, S. & W. and other revolvers; Colt Automatic, Reising and other automatic pistols.

Semi-Smokeless powder, per 1,000	$ 7.00
Hollow Point, Semi-Smokeless, per 1,000	7.60

    Weight of bullet, 40 grains; Hollow Point, 38 grains.
    Packed 50 in a box, 10M in a case.

Semi-Smokeless cartridges are regular, and will be sent unless Smokeless are specified.

RIM FIRE CARTRIDGES

.22 LONG RIFLE INDOOR TACK-HOLE

For extreme accurate shooting up to 75 feet. Adapted to Marlin, Winchester, Remington Auto Loading Mod. 24 and Savage Repeating rifles; Remington, B. S. A., Savage, Stevens, Winchester, Iver-Johnson and other single shot rifles. This cartridge is not designed for use in pistols or revolvers.

Semi-Smokeless powder, per 1,000 .... $ 8.75
    Weight of bullet, 40 grains.
    Packed 50 in a box, 10M in a case.

.22 LONG RIFLE OUTDOOR TACK-HOLE

For extreme accurate shooting up to 250 yards. Adapted to Winchester, Marlin, Remington Auto Loading Mod. 24 and Savage Repeating rifles; Remington, B. S. A., Savage, Stevens, Winchester, Iver-Johnson and other single shot rifles; Colt, S. & W. and other revolvers; Colt Automatic, Reising and other automatic pistols.

Semi-Smokeless powder, per 1,000 .... $ 8.75
    Weight of bullet, 40 grains.
    Packed 50 in a box, 10M in a case.

.22 EXTRA LONG

Adapted to old Remington, Ballard, Stevens, Wesson, and other single shot rifles; also S. & W. revolvers.

Semi-Smokeless powder, per 1,000 .... $10.50
    Weight of bullet, 40 grains.
    Packed 50 in a box, 10M in a case.

Semi-Smokeless cartridges are regular, and will be sent unless Smokeless are specified.

RIM FIRE CARTRIDGES

.22 WINCHESTER R. F.   .22 WINCHESTER R. F. HOLLOW POINT

Adapted to Winchester Model 1890 and Remington Model 12 Hammerless Repeating rifles; Remington, Winchester, Stevens single shot rifles; also Colt target revolvers.

Semi-Smokeless powder, per 1,000 $10.50
Smokeless powder, lubricated bullet, per 1,000   11.75
Smokeless powder, non-lubricated, per 1,000   11.75
     Weight of bullet, 46 grains.
Hollow Point, Semi-Smokeless powder, per 1,000   11.00
Hollow Point, Smokeless powder, lubricated, per 1,000   12.25
     Weight of bullet, 44 grains.
     Packed 50 in a box, 5M in a case.

.22 WINCHESTER AUTOMATIC   .22 WINCHESTER AUTO. HOLLOW POINT

Adapted to Winchester Automatic Rifle, Model 1903.

Smokeless powder, per 1,000 $11.75
     Weight of bullet, 45 grains.
Hollow Point, Smokeless powder, per 1,000   12.25
     Weight of bullet, 44 grains.
     Packed 50 in a box, 5M in a case.

.22 REMINGTON AUTO. LOADING   .22 REMINGTON AUTO. LOADING HOLLOW POINT

Adapted to Remington Auto Loading Rifles, Model 16.

Smokeless powder, per 1,000 $11.75
     Weight of bullet, 47 grains.
Hollow Point, Smokeless powder, per 1,000   12.25
     Weight of bullet, 45 grains.
     Packed 50 in a box, 5M in a case.

     Semi-Smokeless cartridges are regular, and will be sent unless Smokeless are specified.

RIM FIRE CARTRIDGES

.25 SHORT STEVENS

Adapted to Winchester, Remington and Marlin single shot rifles.

Semi-Smokeless, per 1,000 .... $11.75
    Weight of bullet, 68 grains.
    Packed 50 in a box, 4M in a case.

.25 STEVENS   .25 STEVENS HOLLOW POINT

    Adapted to Stevens, Marlin, Remington and Winchester single shot rifles; also Stevens Model 80, and Marlin Repeating rifles.

Semi-Smokeless powder, per 1,000 .... $16.50
    Weight of bullet, 68 grains.
Hollow Point, Semi-Smokeless powder, per 1,000 .... 17.00
    Weight of bullet, 65 grains.
    Packed 50 in a box, 2M in a case.

.32 EXTRA SHORT

    Adapted to Remington and Protector Repeating pistols. Can also be used in .32 caliber Rim Fire arms.

Semi-Smokeless powder, per 1,000 .... $11.75
    Weight of bullet, 55 grains.
    Packed 50 in a box, 5M in a case.

RIM FIRE CARTRIDGES

.32 SHORT

Adapted to Winchester, Remington, Ballard, Wesson, Whitney, Stevens, Forehand and Wadsworth, and other single shot rifles; Marlin Repeating rifles, Model 1892; Colt and other revolvers and single shot pistols; also rifle canes.

Semi-Smokeless powder, per 1,000 .... $11.75
    Weight of bullet, 82 grains.
    Packed 50 in a box, 5M in a case.

.32 LONG

Adapted to Winchester, Remington, Ballard, Wesson, Whitney, Stevens, Forehand and Wadsworth, and other single shot rifles; Marlin Repeating rifles, Model 1892; Colt and other revolvers and single shot pistols; also rifle canes.

Semi-Smokeless powder, per 1,000 .... $13.50
    Weight of bullet, 90 grains.
    Packed 50 in a box, 5M in a case.

.38 SHORT

Adapted to Remington, Ballard, Forehand and Wadsworth, Wesson and other rifles; also revolvers of this caliber.

Semi-Smokeless powder, per 1,000 .... $18.75
    Weight of bullet, 125 grains.
    Packed 50 in a box, 3M in a case.

RIM FIRE CARTRIDGES

.41 SHORT

Adapted to National, Williamson, Colt, Remington, Southern Derringer, Forehand and Wadsworth, and other pistols.

Semi-Smokeless powder, per 1,000.. **$17.50**
    Weight of bullet, 130 grains.
    Packed 50 in a box, 3M in a case.

.41 SWISS

Adapted to Swiss, Vetterli and other rifles.

Smokeless powder, per 1,000.. **$57.00**
    Weight of bullet, 300 grains.
    Packed 20 in a box, 1M in a case.

CENTER FIRE CARTRIDGES
PISTOL, REVOLVER AND RIFLE

5.5 m/m VELO DOG

Adapted to Velo Dog revolvers.

Smokeless powder, metal case bullet, per 1,000 .... $26.25
   Primer, Peters No. 1½. Weight of bullet, 45 grains.
   Packed 25 in a box, 2M in a case.

.22 WINCHESTER CENTER FIRE

Adapted to Winchester, Stevens, Remington and other single shot rifles.

Semi-Smokeless powder, per 1,000 .... $26.25
Smokeless powder, lead bullet, per 1,000 .... 29.75
   Primer, Peters No. 1. Weight of bullet, 46 grains.
   Packed 50 in a box, 2M in a case.

.25-20 WINCHESTER AND MARLIN

Adapted to Winchester Model '92, Marlin Models 1894 and 27, Savage Model 23-B, and Remington Model 25 repeating rifles.

Semi-Smokeless powder, lead bullet, per 1,000 .... $28.00
Smokeless powder, lead bullet, per 1,000 .... 33.25
Smokeless powder, metal case bullet, per 1,000 .... 35.00
Smokeless powder, soft point bullet, per 1,000 .... 35.00
   Primer, Peters No. 1. Weight of bullet, 86 grains.
   Packed 50 in a box, 2M in a case.

Smokeless powder cartridges supplied with Lead Bullets unless otherwise specified.

CENTER FIRE CARTRIDGES
PISTOL-REVOLVER-RIFLE

.25-20 WINCHESTER AND MARLIN—HIGH VELOCITY

Adapted to Winchester Model '92, Marlin Models 1894 and 27, Savage Model 23-B and Remington Model 25 repeating rifles.

Smokeless powder, soft point bullet, per 1,000 .... **$36.75**
    Primer, Peters No. 6½.   Weight of bullet, 86 grains.
    Packed 50 in a box, 2M in a case.

.25-20 WINCHESTER AND MARLIN HIGH VELOCITY EXPANDING

Adapted to Winchester Model '92, Marlin Models 1894 and 27, Savage Model 23-B and Remington Model 25 repeating rifles.

Smokeless powder, expanding point bullet, per 1,000 .... **$35.00**
    Primer, Peters No. 6½.   Weight of bullet, 60 grains.
    Packed 50 in a box, 2M in a case.

.25-20 SINGLE SHOT

Adapted to Winchester, Maynard, Remington, Stevens and other single shot rifles.

Semi-Smokeless powder, per 1,000 .... **$31.50**
Smokeless powder, lead bullet, per 1,000 .... **36.75**
Smokeless powder, metal case bullet, per 1,000 .... **38.50**
Smokeless powder, soft point bullet, per 1,000 .... **38.50**
    Primer, Peters No. 1.   Weight of bullet, 86 grains.
    Packed 50 in a box, 2M in a case.

Smokeless powder cartridges supplied with Lead Bullets unless otherwise specified.

CENTER FIRE CARTRIDGES
PISTOL-REVOLVER-RIFLE

.25 AUTOMATIC PISTOL (6.35 m/m)

Adapted to Browning, Colt, Mauser, Clement, Webley & Scott, Steyr, Pieper, and H. & R. automatic pistols.

Smokeless powder, metal case bullet, per 1,000	$29.00
Smokeless powder, soft point bullet, per 1,000	29.00

Primer, Peters No. 1½. Weight of bullet, 50 grains.
Packed 50 in a box, 5M in a case.

.30 LUGER (7.65 m/m)

Adapted to Luger and Parabellum automatic pistols. Not for use in Luger carbine.

Smokeless powder, metal case bullet, per 1,000	$45.50
Smokeless powder, soft point bullet, per 1,000	45.50
Smokeless powder, hollow point bullet, per 1,000	45.50

Primer, Peters No. 1½. Weight of bullet, 93 grains.
Packed 50 in a box, 2M in a case.

.32 SHORT COLT

Adapted to Colt, Webley, Tranter, and other double action revolvers; also Marlin Model 1892 repeating rifle.

Semi-Smokeless powder, per 1,000	$19.25
Smokeless powder, per 1,000	21.00

Primer, Peters No. 1½. Weight of bullet, 82 grains.
Packed 50 in a box, 5M in a case.

Smokeless powder cartridges supplied with Lead Bullets unless otherwise specified.

CENTER FIRE CARTRIDGES
PISTOL-REVOLVER-RIFLE

.32 LONG COLT

Adapted to Colt, Webley, Tranter and other revolvers; also rifles of this caliber.

Semi-Smokeless powder, per 1,000	$21.00
Smokeless powder, per 1,000	23.50

Primer, Peters No. 1½. Weight of bullet, 82 grains.
Packed 50 in a box, 5M in a case.

.32 COLT NEW POLICE (POL. POS.)

Adapted to .32 Colt New Police and Police Positive and S. & W. Hand-Ejector revolvers.

Semi-Smokeless powder, per 1,000	$21.00
Smokeless powder, lead bullet, per 1,000	23.50
Smokeless powder, metal point bullet, per 1,000	25.50

Primer, Peters No. 1½. Weight of lead bullet, 100 grains; metal point bullet, 96 grains.

Packed 50 in a box, 5M in a case.

.32 COLT NEW POLICE MID-RANGE (POL. POS.)

Adapted to Colt New Police Double Action and Smith & Wesson Hand Ejector revolvers.

Smokeless powder, per 1,000	$20.00

Primer, Peters No. 1½. Weight of lead bullet, 100 grains.
Packed 50 in a box, 5M in a case.

Smokeless powder cartridges supplied with Lead Bullets unless otherwise specified.

CENTER FIRE CARTRIDGES
PISTOL-REVOLVER-RIFLE

.32 AUTOMATIC PISTOL (7.65 m/m)

Adapted to Colt, Remington Model 51, Savage, H. & R., Webley & Scott, Mauser, Clement, Browning, Frommer, Steyr, Pieper and Schwartz-Lose automatic pistols.

Smokeless powder, metal case bullet, per 1,000	$31.50
Smokeless powder, soft point bullet, per 1,000	31.50

Primer, Peters No. 1½. Weight of bullet, 73 grains.
Packed 50 in a box, 5M in a case.

.32 SMITH & WESSON

Adapted to S. & W., Colt New Police, Iver-Johnson, H. & R. and H. & A. revolvers.

Semi-Smokeless powder, per 1,000	$19.25
Smokeless powder, lead bullet, per 1,000	21.00
Smokeless powder, metal point bullet, per 1,000	22.75

Primer, Peters No. 1½. Weight of bullet, 86 grains.
Packed 50 in a box, 5M in a case.

.32 SMITH & WESSON LONG

Adapted to .32 S. & W. Hand-Ejector, Colt New Police (Police Positive) and H. & R. revolvers.

Semi-Smokeless powder, per 1,000	$21.00
Smokeless powder, lead bullet, per 1,000	23.50
Smokeless powder, metal point bullet, per 1,000	25.50

Primer, Peters No. 1½. Weight of bullet, 98 grains.
Packed 50 in a box, 5M in a case.

Smokeless powder cartridges supplied with Lead Bullets unless otherwise specified.

CENTER FIRE CARTRIDGES
PISTOL-REVOLVER-RIFLE

.32 WINCHESTER C. F. (.32-20)

Adapted to Winchester Models 1873 and 1892; Remington Model 25, Marlin Models 1894 and 27, Savage Model 23-C and Colt repeating rifles; Remington and Winchester single shot rifles; also Colt and S. & W. revolvers.

Semi-Smokeless powder, lead bullet, per 1,000	**$28.00**
Smokeless powder, lead bullet, per 1,000	33.25
Smokeless powder, metal case bullet, per 1,000	35.00
Smokeless powder, soft point bullet, per 1,000	35.00

Primer, Peters No. 1. Weight of bullet, 100 grains.
Packed 50 in a box, 2M in a case.

.32 WINCHESTER, C. F., HIGH VELOCITY (.32-20)

Adapted to Winchester Model 1892 and Marlin Model 1894, Savage Model 23-C and Remington Model 25 repeating rifles; also single shot rifles. Not for use in revolvers.

Smokeless powder, soft point bullet, per 1,000 .... **$36.75**

Primer, Peters No. 6½. Weight of bullet, 100 grains.
Packed 50 in a box, 2M in a case.

.32 WINCHESTER, C. F., HIGH VELOCITY, EXPANDING (.32-20)

Adapted to Winchester Model 1892 and Marlin Model 1894, Savage Model 23-C and Remington Model 25 repeating rifles; also single shot rifles. Not for use in revolvers.

Smokeless powder, expanding point bullet, per 1,000 .... **$35.00**

Primer, Peters No. 6½. Weight of bullet, 80 grains.
Packed 50 in a box, 2M in a case.

Smokeless powder cartridges supplied with Lead Bullets unless otherwise specified.

CENTER FIRE CARTRIDGES
PISTOL-REVOLVER-RIFLE

9 m/m LUGER

Adapted to Luger Automatic pistols.

Smokeless powder, metal case bullet, per 1,000	$47.25
Smokeless powder, hollow point bullet, per 1,000	47.25

Primer, Peters No. 1. Weight of bullet, 125 grains.
Packed 50 in a box, 2M in a case.

.35 S. & W. AUTOMATIC

Adapted to Smith & Wesson Automatic pistols of this caliber.

Smokeless powder, soft point bullet, per 1,000	$31.50
Smokeless powder, metal point bullet, per 1,000	31.50

Primer, Peters No. 1½. Weight of bullet, 76 grains.
Packed 50 in a box, 5M in a case.

.38 SMITH & WESSON

Adapted to S. & W., Colt New Police, H. & R., H. & A., Iver-Johnson revolvers.

Semi-Smokeless powder, per 1,000	$23.50
Smokeless powder, lead bullet, per 1,000	27.25
Smokeless powder, metal point bullet, per 1,000	29.00

Primer, Peters No. 1½. Weight of bullet, 146 grains.
Packed 50 in a box, 2M in a case.

Smokeless powder cartridges supplied with Lead Bullets unless otherwise specified.

CENTER FIRE CARTRIDGES
PISTOL-REVOLVER-RIFLE

.38 S. & W. SPECIAL

Adapted to S. & W. New Military and Police revolver, Colt D. A., Colt Army Special and Colt Police Positive Special revolvers, and Colt Officers' model.

Semi-Smokeless powder, per 1,000	$29.00
Smokeless powder, lead bullet, per 1,000	32.50
Smokeless powder, metal point bullet, per 1,000	34.00

Primer, Peters No. 1½. Weight of bullet, 158 grains.
Packed 50 in a box, 2M in a case.

.38 S. & W. SPECIAL WAD CUTTER

Adapted to S. & W. New Military and Police revolver, Colt D. A., Colt Army Special and Colt Police Positive Special revolvers, and Colt Officers' model.

Smokeless powder, per 1,000 .... $32.50
Primer, Peters No. 1½. Weight of bullet, 147 grains.
Packed 50 in a box, 2M in a case.

.38 S. & W. SPECIAL MID-RANGE WAD CUTTER

Adapted to Smith & Wesson New Military revolver and Colt Police Special and Army Special revolvers, and Colt Officers' model.

Smokeless powder, per 1,000 .... $28.00
Primer, Peters No. 1½. Weight of bullet, 147 grains.
Packed 50 in a box, 2M in a case.

Smokeless powder cartridges supplied with Lead Bullets unless otherwise specified.

CENTER FIRE CARTRIDGES
PISTOL-REVOLVER-RIFLE

.38 S. & W. SPECIAL GALLERY

Adapted to Smith & Wesson New Military revolvers, Colt Police Special and Army Special revolvers, and Colt Officers' model.

Semi-Smokeless powder, per 1,000 .... $25.50
    Primer, Peters No. 1½. Weight of bullet, 115 grains.
    Packed 50 in a box, 2M in a case.

.38 COLT NEW POLICE (POLICE POSITIVE)

Adapted to S. & W. New Military and Police revolver, Colt D. A., Colt Army Special and Colt Police Positive Special revolvers.

Semi-Smokeless powder, per 1,000 .... $23.50
Smokeless powder, lead bullet, per 1,000 .... 27.25
    Primer, Peters No. 1½. Weight of lead bullet, 150 grains.
    Packed 50 in a box, 2M in a case.

.38 SHORT COLT

Adapted to S. & W. New Military and Police revolvers, Colt D. A., Colt Army Special and Colt Police Positive Special revolvers.

Semi-Smokeless powder, per 1,000 .... $23.50
Smokeless powder, per 1,000 .... 27.25
    Primer, Peters No. 1½. Weight of bullet, 125 grains.
    Packed 50 in a box, 4M in a case.

Smokeless powder cartridges supplied with Lead Bullets unless otherwise specified.

CENTER FIRE CARTRIDGES
PISTOL-REVOLVER-RIFLE

.38 LONG COLT, D. A.

Adapted to S. & W. New Military and Police revolver, Colt D. A., Colt Army Special and Colt Police Positive Special revolvers.

Semi-Smokeless powder, per 1,000	$25.50
Smokeless powder, lead bullet, per 1,000	29.00
Smokeless powder, metal point bullet, per 1,000	30.75

Primer, Peters No. 1½. Weight of bullet, 150 grains; M. P., 148 grains.
Packed 50 in a box, 3M in a case.

.38 LONG COLT, D. A., MID-RANGE

Adapted to S. & W. New Military and Police revolver, Colt D. A., Colt Army Special and Colt Police Positive Special revolvers.

Smokeless powder, lead bullet, per 1,000	$24.50

Primer, Peters No. 1½. Weight of bullet, 150 grains.
Packed 50 in a box, 3M in a case.

.38 COLT SPECIAL

Adapted to Colt Army Special and Smith & Wesson New Military revolvers and Colt Officers' Model

Semi-Smokeless powder, per 1,000	$29.00
Smokeless powder, lead bullet, per 1,000	32.50

Primer, Peters No. 1½. Weight of bullet, 158 grains.
Packed 50 in a box, 2M in a case.

Smokeless powder cartridges supplied with Lead Bullets unless otherwise specified.

CENTER FIRE CARTRIDGES
PISTOL-REVOLVER-RIFLE

.38 AUTOMATIC PISTOL

Adapted to Colt Automatic pistols.

Smokeless powder, metal case bullet, per 1,000	$45.50
Smokeless powder, soft point bullet, per 1,000	45.50

Primer, Peters No. 1½. Weight of bullet, 130 grains.
Packed 50 in a box, 2M in a case.

.380 (9 m/m) AUTOMATIC PISTOL

Adapted to Colt Automatic Hammerless, Remington Model 51, Savage, Webley and 9 m/m Browning (Short) automatic pistols.

Smokeless powder, metal case bullet, per 1,000	$43.75
Smokeless powder, soft point bullet, per 1,000	43.75

Primer, Peters No. 1½. Weight of bullet, 95 grains.
Packed 50 in a box, 2M in a case.

.38 WINCHESTER C. F. (38-40)

Adapted to Marlin, Winchester Models 1873 and 1892, Remington Model 14½, and Colt repeating rifles; Remington, Winchester single shot rifles; also Colt and Smith & Wesson revolvers.

Semi-Smokeless powder, lead bullet, per 1,000	$33.25
Smokeless powder, metal case bullet, per 1,000	42.00
Smokeless powder, soft point bullet, per 1,000	42.00

Primer, Peters No. 1. Weight of bullet, 180 grains.
Packed 50 in a box, 2M in a case.

Smokeless powder cartridges supplied with Lead Bullets unless otherwise specified.

CENTER FIRE CARTRIDGES
PISTOL-REVOLVER-RIFLE

.38 WINCHESTER AND MARLIN C. F., HIGH VELOCITY (.38-40)

Adapted to Marlin Model 1894, Winchester Model 1892, Remington Model 14½ repeating rifles; also single shot rifles. Not for use in revolvers.

Smokeless powder, soft point bullet, per 1,000 .... $47.25
    Primer, Peters No. 6½. Weight of bullet, 180 grains.
    Packed 50 in a box, 2M in a case.

.41 SHORT COLT, D. A.

Adapted to Colt Double Action and Frontier Model Single Action revolvers.

Semi-Smokeless powder, per 1,000 .... $26.25
Smokeless powder, per 1,000 .... 29.75
    Primer, Peters No. 1½. Weight of bullet, 160 grains.
    Packed 50 in a box, 2M in a case.

.41 LONG COLT, D. A.

Adapted to Colt Double Action and Frontier Model Single Action revolvers.

Semi-Smokeless powder, per 1,000 .... $30.75
Smokeless powder, per 1,000 .... 35.00
    Primer, Peters No. 1½. Weight of bullet, 195 grains.
    Packed 50 in a box, 2M in a case.

Smokeless powder cartridges supplied with Lead Bullets unless otherwise specified.

CENTER FIRE CARTRIDGES
PISTOL-REVOLVER-RIFLE

.44 S. & W. AMERICAN

Adapted to Smith & Wesson (old) American Model, Army and Navy revolver, and Merwin, Hulbert & Co. Army revolver.

Semi-Smokeless powder, per 1,000 .... $33.25
    Primer, Peters No. 2X. Weight of bullet, 205 grains.
    Packed 50 in a box, 2M in a case.

.44 S. & W. RUSSIAN

Adapted to S. & W. Russian and Special Models, Colt New Service revolvers; also Remington single shot target pistol and Colt S. A. Army model.

Semi-Smokeless powder, per 1,000 .... $35.00
Smokeless powder, lead bullet, per 1,000 .... 38.50
    Primer, Peters No. 2X. Weight of bullet, 246 grains.
    Packed 50 in a box, 2M in a case.

.44 S. & W. SPECIAL

Adapted to .44 Smith & Wesson Special revolver.

Semi-Smokeless powder, per 1,000 .... $38.50
Smokeless powder, lead bullet, per 1,000 .... 42.00
Smokeless powder, metal point bullet, per 1,000 .... 43.75
    Primer, Peters No. 2X. Weight of bullet, 246 grains.
    Packed 50 in a box, 2M in a case.

Smokeless powder cartridges supplied with Lead Bullets unless otherwise specified.

CENTER FIRE CARTRIDGES
PISTOL-REVOLVER-RIFLE

.44 WINCHESTER AND MARLIN C. F. (44-40)

Adapted to Winchester Models 1873 and 1892, Remington Model 14½, Marlin, Colt, and other repeating rifles; Remington, Winchester, and other single shot rifles; also to Colt, Smith & Wesson, Merwin, Hulbert & Co., Remington and other revolvers.

Semi-Smokeless powder, lead bullet, per 1,000	$33.25
Smokeless powder, metal case bullet, per 1,000	42.00
Smokeless powder, soft point bullet, per 1,000	42.00
Semi-Smokeless powder, hollow point, per 1,000	34.00

Primer, Peters No. 1. Weight of bullet, 200 grains; Hollow Point, 165 grains. Packed 50 in a box, 2M in a case.

.44 WINCHESTER AND MARLIN C. F., HIGH VELOCITY (44-40)

Adapted to Winchester Model 1892, Remington Model 14½ and Marlin Model 1894 repeating rifles; also to single shot rifles. Not for use in revolvers.

Smokeless powder, soft point bullet, per 1,000	$47.25

Primer, Peters No. 6½. Weight of bullet, 200 grains. Packed 50 in a box, 2M in a case.

.44 WEBLEY

Adapted to Webley, Bull Dog and other double action revolvers.

Semi-Smokeless powder, per 1,000	$29.00

Primer, Peters No. 2X. Weight of bullet, 200 grains. Packed 50 in a box, 2M in a case.

Smokeless powder cartridges supplied with Lead Bullets unless otherwise specified.

CENTER FIRE CARTRIDGES
PISTOL-REVOLVER-RIFLE

.44 BULL DOG

Adapted to Webley, American and British Bull Dog revolvers.

Semi-Smokeless powder, per 1,000 ... **$25.50**
    Primer, Peters No. 2X. Weight of bullet, 168 grains.
    Packed 50 in a box, 2M in a case.

.44 GAME GETTER

Adapted to Marble Game Getter and other smooth bore rifles and shot guns.

Semi-Smokeless powder, per 1,000 ... **$33.25**
Smokeless powder, per 1,000 ... **38.50**
    Primer, Peters No. 1. Weight of bullet, 119 grains.
    Packed 50 in a box, 2M in a case.

.45 COLT

Adapted to Colt Single and Double Action Army and New Service revolvers.

Semi-Smokeless powder, lead bullet, per 1,000 ... **$38.50**
Smokeless powder, lead bullet, per 1,000 ... **43.00**
    Primer, Peters No. 2X. Weight of bullet, 255 grains.
    Packed 50 in a box, 2M in a case.

Smokeless powder cartridges supplied with Lead Bullets unless otherwise specified.

CENTER FIRE CARTRIDGES
PISTOL-REVOLVER-RIFLE

.45 COLT AUTOMATIC

Adapted to Colt Automatic Pistol and Thompson Sub-Machine Gun; also S. & W. and Colt 1917 D. A. Revolver, with use of clips.

Smokeless powder, metal case bullet, per 1,000 .... $52.50
    Primer, Peters No. 2X. Weight of bullet, 200 grains.
    Packed 50 in a box, 2M in a case.

.45 COLT AUTOMATIC, GOVERNMENT MODEL

Adapted to Colt Automatic Pistol, Government Model, and Thompson Sub-Machine Gun; also S. & W. and Colt 1917 D. A. revolver, with the use of clips.

Smokeless powder, metal case bullet, per 1,000 .... $52.50
    Primer, Peters No. 2X. Weight of bullet, 230 grains.
    Packed 50 in a box, 2M in a case.

.45 AUTO RIM

Adapted to Smith & Wesson and Colt Model 1917 D. A. revolver, chambered for .45 Automatic Ammunition, eliminating the use of clips.

Smokeless powder, metal case bullet, per 1,000 .... $52.50
    Weight of bullet, 230 grains.
    Packed 50 in a box, 2M in a case.
Smokeless powder, lead bullet, per 1,000 .... $51.00
    Primer, Peters No. 2X. Weight of bullet, 255 grains.
    Packed 50 in a box, 2M in a case.

    Smokeless powder cartridges supplied with Lead Bullets unless otherwise specified.

CENTER FIRE CARTRIDGES
MILITARY AND SPORTING

7 m/m MAUSER

Adapted to Mauser rifles, Spanish and Brazilian Models, Remington and Remington-Lee Military and Sporting Arms; Colt, and other Automatic Machine guns.

Smokeless powder, metal case bullet, per 1,000	**$95.00**
Smokeless powder, soft point bullet, per 1,000	95.00

Primer, Peters No. 11. Weight of bullet, 175 grains.
Packed 20 in a box, 1M in a case.

7.65 m/m MAUSER

Adapted to Mauser rifles, Belgian and Argentine Models, Remington and Remington-Lee Military and Sporting Arms; Colt and other Automatic Machine guns.

Smokeless powder, metal case bullet, per 1,000	**$95.00**
Smokeless powder, soft point bullet, per 1,000	95.00

Primer, Peters No. 11. Weight of bullet, 219 grains.
Packed 20 in a box, 1M in a case.

.22 SAVAGE HIGH POWER

Adapted to Savage High Power rifles.

Smokeless powder, soft point bullet, per 1,000	**$72.25**
Smokeless powder, metal case bullet, per 1,000	72.25

Primer, Peters No. 11. Weight of bullet, 70 grains.
Packed 20 in a box, 1M in a case.

Cartridges supplied with Soft Point Bullets unless otherwise specified.

CENTER FIRE CARTRIDGES—MILITARY AND SPORTING

.250-3000 SAVAGE

Adapted to Savage High Power rifles.

Smokeless powder, metal case bullet, per 1,000	$80.00
Smokeless powder, soft point bullet, per 1,000	80.00
Smokeless powder, Protected Point Expanding bullet, per 1,000	82.00

Primer, Peters No. 11½. Weight of bullet, 87 grains.
Packed 20 in a box, 1M in a case.

.25-35 WINCHESTER AND SAVAGE (HIGH VELOCITY)

Adapted to Winchester Model 1894, Savage, and other repeating rifles.

Smokeless powder, metal case bullet, per 1,000	$62.75
Smokeless powder, soft point bullet, per 1,000	62.75

Primer, Peters No. 11. Weight of bullet, 117 grains.
Packed 20 in a box, 1M in a case.

25-36 MARLIN

Adapted to Marlin 1893 repeating rifles.

Smokeless powder, soft point bullet, per 1,000	$62.75

Primer, Peters No. 11. Weight of bullet, 117 grains.
Packed 20 in a box, 1M in a case.

Cartridges supplied with Soft Point Bullets unless otherwise specified.

CENTER FIRE CARTRIDGES—MILITARY AND SPORTING

.25 REMINGTON (HIGH VELOCITY)

Adapted to Remington Auto Loading or Repeating and Rem. Model 30 bolt action, Standard Automatic and Stevens Repeating rifles.

Smokeless powder, metal case bullet, per 1,000	$62.75
Smokeless powder, soft point bullet, per 1,000	62.75

Primer, Peters No. 11½. Weight of bullet, 117 grains.
Packed 20 in a box, 1M in a case.

.270 WINCHESTER

Adapted to Winchester Rifle, Model 54.

Smokeless powder, Protected Point Expanding bullet, per 1,000 .... $106.50
Primer, Peters No. 11. Weight of bullet, 130 grains.
Packed 20 in a box, 1M in a case.

.30-30 WINCHESTER AND MARLIN (HIGH VELOCITY)

Adapted to Winchester Model 1894, Marlin Model 1893, Remington-Lee, Savage Repeating and Remington No. 5 rifle.

Smokeless powder, metal case bullet, per 1,000	$72.25
Smokeless powder, soft point bullet, per 1,000	72.25
Smokeless powder, M. C. Exp. Hol. Pt., per 1,000	72.25

Primer, Peters No. 11. Weight of bullet: S. P., 170 grs.; M. C., 160 grs.
  M. C. Exp. Hol. Pt., 125 grs. and 165 grs.
Packed 20 in a box, 1M in a case.
In ordering M. C. Exp. Hol. Pt., specify bullet weight.

Cartridges supplied with Soft Point Bullets unless otherwise specified.

CENTER FIRE CARTRIDGES—MILITARY AND SPORTING

.30 REMINGTON

Adapted to Remington Auto Loading or Repeating and Rem. Model 30 bolt action, Standard Automatic and Stevens Repeating rifles.

Smokeless powder, metal case bullet, per 1,000	$72.25
Smokeless powder, soft point bullet, per 1,000	72.25
Smokeless powder, M. C. Exp. Hol. Pt., per 1,000	72.25

    Primer, Peters No. 11½. Weight of bullet: S. P., 170 grs.; M. C., 160 grs.; M. C. Exp. Hol. Pt., 125 grs. and 165 grs.
    Packed 20 in a box, 1M in a case.
    In ordering M. C. Exp. Hol. Pt., specify bullet weight.

.30-40 KRAG U. S. ARMY ROUND NOSE BULLET

Adapted to U. S. Krag, Remington-Lee and Winchester 1895 rifles; also to Remington and Winchester Single Shot Military and Sporting rifles.

Smokeless powder, metal case bullet, per 1,000	$95.00
Smokeless powder, soft point bullet, per 1,000	95.00

    Primer, Peters No. 11. Weight of bullet, 220 grains.
    Packed 20 in a box, 1M in a case.

.30-40 KRAG U. S. ARMY POINTED BULLET

Adapted to U. S. Krag, Remington-Lee and Winchester 1895 rifles; also to Remington and Winchester Single Shot Military and Sporting rifles

Smokeless powder, soft point bullet, 150 grs., per 1,000	$95.00
Smokeless powder, soft point bullet, 180 grs., per 1,000	95.00
Smokeless powder, Protected Point Expdg. bullet, 180 grs., per 1,000	97.00
Smokeless powder, Protected Point Expdg. bullet, 150 grs., per 1,000	97.00

    Primer, Peters No. 11.
    Packed 20 in a box, 1M in a case.

    Cartridges supplied with Soft Point Bullets unless otherwise specified.

CENTER FIRE CARTRIDGES—MILITARY AND SPORTING

.30 GOVERNMENT 1903

Adapted to 1903 Model U. S. Springfield Magazine rifle, chambered for 1903 cartridge, and Winchester Model 1895.

Smokeless powder, metal case bullet, per 1,000	**$104.50**
Smokeless powder, soft point bullet, per 1,000	104.50

Primer, Peters No. 11.   Weight of bullet, 220 grains.
Packed 20 in a box, 1M in a case.

.30 GOVERNMENT 1906

Adapted to Model 1903, U. S. Springfield Magazine rifle, chambered for 1906 cartridges, and Winchester Rifle Model 1895; Winchester Rifle Model 54. Also to Remington Model 30 bolt action rifle.

Smokeless powder, metal case 150 gr. bullet, per 1,000	**$104.50**
Smokeless powder, soft point 150 gr. bullet, per 1,000	104.50
Smokeless powder, Protected Point Expanding bullet, 150 gr., per 1,000	106.50
Smokeless powder, metal case, 180 gr. bullet, per 1,000	104.50
Smokeless powder, soft point, 180 gr. bullet, per 1,000	104.50
Smokeless powder, Protected Point Expanding bullet, 180 gr., per 1,000	106.50
Smokeless powder, soft point, round nose bullet, 220 gr., per 1,000	104.50

Primer, Peters No. 11.
Packed 20 in a box, 1M in a case.

.300 SAVAGE

Adapted to .300 Savage Repeating rifle.

Smokeless powder, Protected Point Expanding bullet, per 1,000	**$92.00**

Primer, Peters No. 11½.   Weight of bullet, 150 grains.
Packed 20 in a box, 1M in a case.

Cartridges supplied with Soft Point Bullets unless otherwise specified.

CENTER FIRE CARTRIDGES—MILITARY AND SPORTING

.303 BRITISH (MARK VI) ROUND NOSE BULLET

Adapted to Lee-Metford, Lee Enfield and Winchester Model '95, Remington and Ross Repeating rifles.

Smokeless powder, metal case bullet, per 1,000	$95.00
Smokeless powder, soft point bullet, per 1,000	95.00

Primer, Peters No. 11. Weight of bullet, 215 grains.
Packed 20 in a box, 1M in a case.

.303 SAVAGE

Adapted to .303 Savage Rifle, Model 1899.

Smokeless powder, metal case bullet, per 1,000	$72.25
Smokeless powder, soft point bullet, per 1,000	72.25

Primer, Peters No. 11. Weight of bullet, 190 grains.
Packed 20 in a box, 1M in a case.

8 m/m MAUSER (7.9 m/m)

Adapted to Mauser, Sauer-Mauser and Schilling-Mauser Model 1888; Haenel, Mannlicher, Model 1888, and Mannlicher Schoenauer, Model 1908, Military and Sporting rifles.

Smokeless powder, metal case bullet, per 1,000	$95.00
Smokeless powder, soft point bullet, per 1,000	95.00

Primer, Peters No. 11. Weight of bullet: S. P., 170 grs.; M. C., 227 grs.
Packed 20 in a box, 1M in a case.

Cartridges supplied with Soft Point Bullets unless otherwise specified.

CENTER FIRE CARTRIDGES—MILITARY AND SPORTING

8 m/m MANNLICHER SCHOENAUER

Adapted to Mannlicher Schoenauer Rifle Model 1908.

Smokeless powder, soft point bullet, 200 grs., per 1,000	$95.00
Smokeless powder, metal case bullet, 227 grs., per 1,000	95.00

Primer, Peters No. 11.
Packed 20 in a box, 1M in a case.

.32 WINCHESTER SPECIAL

Adapted to Winchester Model 1894, Marlin Model 1893, and Remington-Lee High Power rifles; also Remington Nos. 3 and 5 High Power rifles.

Smokeless powder, metal case bullet, per 1,000	$72.25
Smokeless powder, soft point bullet, per 1,000	72.25

Primer, Peters No. 11. Weight of bullet, 165 grains.
Packed 20 in a box, 1M in a case.

.32 WINCHESTER SELF LOADING

Adapted to Winchester Model 1905 Self Loading rifle.

Smokeless powder, metal case bullet, per 1,000	$51.25
Smokeless powder, soft point bullet, per 1,000	51.25

Primer, Peters No. 6½. Weight of bullet, 165 grains.
Packed 50 in a box, 2M in a case.

Cartridges supplied with Soft Point Bullets unless otherwise specified.

CENTER FIRE CARTRIDGES—MILITARY AND SPORTING

.32 REMINGTON

Adapted to Remington Auto Loading or Repeating, and Rem. Model 30 bolt action, Standard Automatic and Stevens Repeating rifles.

Smokeless powder, metal case bullet, per 1,000 .... $72.25
Smokeless powder, soft point bullet, per 1,000 .... 72.25
   Primer, Peters No. 11½. Weight of bullet, 165 grains.
   Packed 20 in a box, 1M in a case.

.32-40 WINCHESTER, MARLIN AND SAVAGE

Adapted to Winchester Model 1894, Marlin and Savage Repeating rifles, Ballard, Remington and Winchester Single Shot rifles.

Semi-Smokeless powder, per 1,000 .... $51.25
Smokeless powder, metal case bullet, per 1,000 .... 60.75
Smokeless powder, soft point bullet, per 1,000 .... 60.75
   Primer, Peters No. 11. Weight of bullet, 165 grains.
   Packed 20 in a box, 1M in a case.

.32-40 WINCHESTER, MARLIN AND SAVAGE HIGH VELOCITY

Adapted to Winchester, Marlin and Savage Repeating rifles; Remington-Lee Repeating, and Remington High Power Single Shot rifles.

Smokeless powder, soft point bullet, per 1,000 .... $72.25
   Primer, Peters No. 11. Weight of bullet, 165 grains.
   Packed 20 in a box, 1M in a case.

Cartridges supplied with Soft Point Bullets unless otherwise specified.

CENTER FIRE CARTRIDGES—MILITARY AND SPORTING

.33 WINCHESTER

Adapted to Winchester Model 1886 Repeating rifle.

Smokeless powder, soft point bullet, per 1,000 .... **$95.00**
   Primer, Peters No. 11.   Weight of bullet, 200 grains.
   Packed 20 in a box, 1M in a case.

.35 WINCHESTER

Adapted to Winchester Model 1895, Remington-Lee and Ross Repeating rifles.

Smokeless powder, soft point bullet, per 1,000 .... **$104.50**
   Primer, Peters No. 11.   Weight of bullet, 250 grains.
   Packed 20 in a box, 1M in a case.

.35 WINCHESTER SELF LOADING

Adapted to Winchester Model 1905 Self Loading rifles.

Smokeless powder, metal case bullet, per 1,000 .... **$52.25**
Smokeless powder, soft point bullet, per 1,000 .... 52.25
   Primer, Peters No. 6½.   Weight of bullet, 180 grains.
   Packed 50 in a box, 2M in a case.

Cartridges supplied with Soft Point Bullets unless otherwise specified.

CENTER FIRE CARTRIDGES—MILITARY AND SPORTING

.35 REMINGTON

Adapted to Remington Auto Loading or Repeating, and Rem. Model 30 bolt action, Standard Automatic and Stevens Repeating rifles.

Smokeless powder, metal case bullet, per 1,000 .... $79.75
Smokeless powder, soft point bullet, per 1,000 .... 79.75
    Primer, Peters No. 11½. Weight of bullet, 200 grains.
    Packed 20 in a box, 1M in a case.

.351 WINCHESTER SELF LOADING

Adapted to Winchester Model 1907 Self Loading rifle.

Smokeless powder, metal case bullet, per 1,000 .... $60.75
Smokeless powder, soft point bullet, per 1,000 .... 60.75
    Primer, Peters No. 6½. Weight of bullet, 180 grains.
    Packed 50 in a box, 2M in a case.

.38-55 WINCHESTER, MARLIN AND SAVAGE

Adapted to Winchester Model 1894, Marlin, Savage and Remington-Lee Repeating rifles; Remington, Ballard and Winchester Single Shot rifles.

Semi-Smokeless powder, per 1,000 .... $62.75
Smokeless powder, metal case bullet, per 1,000 .... 76.00
Smokeless powder, soft point bullet, per 1,000 .... 76.00
    Primer, Peters No. 11. Weight of bullet, 255 grains.
    Packed 20 in a box, 1M in a case.

Cartridges supplied with Soft Point Bullets unless otherwise specified.

CENTER FIRE CARTRIDGES—MILITARY AND SPORTING

.38-55 WINCHESTER, MARLIN AND SAVAGE HIGH VELOCITY

Adapted to Winchester, Marlin, Savage and Remington-Lee Repeating rifles; also Remington High Pressure Single Shot rifles.

Smokeless powder, soft point bullet, per 1,000 .... $87.50
    Primer, Peters No. 11. Weight of bullet, 255 grains.
    Packed 20 in a box, 1M in a case.

.38-56 WINCHESTER AND MARLIN

Adapted to Winchester, Marlin and other Repeating rifles; also to Winchester Single Shot rifles.

Semi-Smokeless powder, per 1,000 .... $62.75
Smokeless powder, soft point bullet, per 1,000 .... 76.00
    Primer, Peters No. 11. Weight of bullet, 255 grains.
    Packed 20 in a box, 1M in a case.

.40-65 WINCHESTER AND MARLIN

Adapted to Winchester Model 1886 and Marlin Repeating rifles; also to Remington and Winchester Single Shot rifles.

Semi-Smokeless powder, per 1,000 .... $62.75
Smokeless powder, soft point bullet, per 1,000 .... 76.00
    Primer, Peters No. 11. Weight of bullet, 260 grains.
    Packed 20 in a box, 1M in a case.

Cartridges supplied with Soft Point Bullets unless otherwise specified.

CENTER FIRE CARTRIDGES—MILITARY AND SPORTING

.40-82 WINCHESTER AND MARLIN

Adapted to Winchester Model 1886 and Marlin Repeating and to Remington and Winchester Single Shot rifles.

Semi-Smokeless powder, per 1,000	$68.50
Smokeless powder, soft point bullet, per 1,000	81.75

Primer, Peters No. 11.   Weight of bullet, 260 grains.
Packed 20 in a box, 1M in a case.

.401 WINCHESTER SELF LOADING

Adapted to Winchester Model 1910 Self Loading rifle.

Smokeless powder, metal case bullet, per 1,000	$76.00
Smokeless powder, soft point bullet, per 1,000	76.00

Primer, Peters No. 11.   Weight of bullet: Metal Case, 200 grains; Soft Point, 200 and 250 grains.
Packed 20 in a box, 1M in a case.
200-grain Soft Point Bullet will be sent unless otherwise specified.

.405 WINCHESTER

Adapted to Winchester Model 1895 Repeating rifle.

Smokeless powder, metal case bullet, per 1,000	$114.00
Smokeless powder, soft point bullet, per 1,000	114.00

Primer, Peters No. 11.   Weight of bullet, 300 grains.
Packed 20 in a box, 1M in a case.

Cartridges supplied with Soft Point Bullets unless otherwise specified.

CENTER FIRE CARTRIDGES—MILITARY AND SPORTING

.45-60 WINCHESTER

Adapted to Winchester Model 1876 and Kennedy Repeating rifles; also Winchester Single Shot rifles.

Semi-Smokeless powder, lead bullet, per 1,000	$62.75

Primer, Peters No. 11. Weight of bullet, 300 grains.
Packed 20 in a box, 1M in a case.

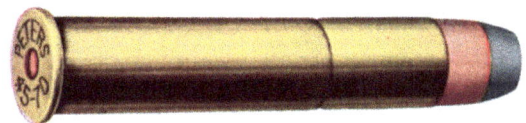

.45-70 GOVERNMENT

Adapted to Springfield, Hotchkiss Repeating rifles; Winchester and Marlin Repeating rifles; Remington and Winchester Single Shot rifles; also Colt and Maxim Machine Guns.

Semi-Smokeless powder, lead bullet, per 1,000	$66.50
Smokeless powder, metal case bullet, per 1,000	79.75
Smokeless powder, soft point bullet, per 1,000	79.75

Primer, Peters No. 11. Weight of bullet, 405 grains.
Packed 20 in a box, 1M in a case.

.45-90 WINCHESTER AND MARLIN

Adapted to Winchester Model 1886 and Marlin Repeating, and to Remington and Winchester Single Shot rifles.

Semi-Smokeless powder, lead bullet, per 1,000	$68.50
Smokeless powder, soft point bullet, per 1,000	81.75

Primer, Peters No. 11. Weight of bullet, 300 grains.
Packed 20 in a box, 1M in a case.

Cartridges supplied with Soft Point Bullets unless otherwise specified.

BLANK CARTRIDGES

RIM FIRE

Peters Blank Cartridges are manufactured under the same high quality standards as all other Peters Cartridges. These Blank Cartridges, used extensively at celebrations and for military purposes, are designed to give an unusually loud, sharp report.

.22 SHORT BLANK

Adapted to Revolver, Single Shot rifles and pistols.

Black powder, per 1,000..$ 3.00
  Packed 50 in a box, 10M in a case.

.32 SHORT BLANK

Adapted to Revolver, Single Shot rifles and pistols.

Black powder, per 1,000..$ 5.50
  Packed 50 in a box, 5M in a case.

BLANK CARTRIDGES
CENTER FIRE

.32 SHORT COLT BLANK

Adapted to Colt, Webley and other revolvers; Marlin rifle, Model 1892.

Black powder, per 1,000..$17.25
    Packed 50 in a box, 5M in a case.

.32 S. & W. BLANK

Adapted to Smith & Wesson, Colt and other revolvers.

Black powder, per 1,000..$11.00
    Packed 50 in a box, 5M in a case.

.38 S. & W. BLANK

Adapted to Smith & Wesson, Colt and other revolvers.

Black powder, per 1,000..$14.00
    Packed 50 in a box, 2M in a case.

BLANK CARTRIDGES—CENTER FIRE

.38 SHORT COLT BLANK

Adapted to Colt and other revolvers; also to rifles.

Black powder, per 1,000...$20.00
   Packed 50 in a box, 4M in a case.

.38 LONG COLT BLANK

Adapted to Colt, Smith & Wesson and other revolvers; also to rifles.

Black powder, per 1,000...$22.75
   Packed 50 in a box, 3M in a case.

.44 WINCHESTER (.44-40) BLANK

Adapted to Winchester Model 1892, Remington Model 14½, and Marlin Model 1894 Repeating rifle; also to Single Shot rifles.

Black powder, per 1,000...$30.00
   Packed 50 in a box, 2M in a case.

BLANK CARTRIDGES—CENTER FIRE

.44 WEBLEY BLANK

Adapted to Webley, Bull Dog and other Double Action revolvers.

Black powder, per 1,000 .... $26.00
    Packed 50 in a box, 2M in a case.

.45 COLT BLANK

Adapted to Colt Single and Double Action Army and New Service revolvers.

Black powder, per 1,000 .... $34.75
    Packed 50 in a box, 2M in a case.

.30-40 BLANK

Adapted to Krag, Winchester Model 1895, Remington-Lee and other rifles.

Smokeless powder, per 1,000 .... $85.50
    Packed 20 in a box, 1M in a case.

BLANK CARTRIDGES—CENTER FIRE

.30 GOVERNMENT 1906 BLANK

Adapted to Springfield Model 1903, chambered for 1906 cartridges; also to Winchester Model 1893 Repeating rifle.

Smokeless powder, per 1,000..$94.00
    Packed 20 in a box, 1M in a case.

.45-70 BLANK

Adapted to Winchester and Marlin Repeating; also to Springfield, Remington and other Single Shot rifles.

Black powder, per 1,000..$60.00
    Packed 20 in a box, 1M in a case.

    All other Blank Cartridges take same list as Ball Cartridges.

RIM FIRE SHOT CARTRIDGES

These cartridges are loaded with small shot, and are unequaled for pattern and penetration, being superior in all respects to any others on the market.

.22 B. B. CAP SHOT

Adapted to Flobert and .22 Caliber Rim Fire Single Shot rifles.

Semi-Smokeless powder, per 1,000...$ 8.00
    Size of shot, No. 12.
    Packed 100 in a box, 10M in a case.

.22 LONG SHOT

Adapted to Remington, Colt, Winchester and Marlin Repeating; also Remington and other Single Shot rifles.

Semi-Smokeless powder, per 1,000...$11.00
Smokeless powder, per 1,000..12.50
    Size of shot, No. 11.
    Packed 50 in a box, 10M in a case.

.32 LONG SHOT

Adapted to Winchester, Remington, Ballard, Wesson, Whitney, Stevens, Forehand and Wadsworth, and other Single Shot rifles; Marlin Repeating rifle, Model 1892; Colt and other revolvers, and other Single Shot pistols.

Semi-Smokeless powder, per 1,000...$22.00
    Size of shot, No. 10.
    Packed 50 in a box, 5M in a case.

RIM FIRE SHOT CARTRIDGES

.41 SWISS SHOT

Adapted to Swiss, Vetterli and other rifles.

Smokeless powder, per 1,000 $57.00
    Size of shot, No. 8.
    Packed 20 in a box, 1M in a case.

CENTER FIRE SHOT CARTRIDGES

.32 S. & W. SHOT

Adapted to S. & W., Colt New Police, Iver-Johnson, H. & R. and H. & A. revolvers.

Semi-Smokeless powder, per 1,000 $18.00
    Size of shot, No. 10.
    Packed 50 in a box, 5M in a case.

.32 WINCHESTER AND MARLIN C. F. SHOT (.32-20)

Adapted to Winchester, Marlin and Colt Repeating rifles; Remington and Winchester Single Shot rifles; also Colt and Smith & Wesson revolvers.

Semi-Smokeless powder, per 1,000 $25.50
    Size of shot, No. 9.
    Packed 50 in a box, 2M in a case.

CENTER FIRE SHOT CARTRIDGES

.38 S. & W. SHOT

Adapted to S. & W., Colt New Police, H. & R., H. & A. and Iver-Johnson revolvers.

Semi-Smokeless powder, per 1,000 .... **$21.75**
    Size of shot, No. 8.
    Packed 50 in a box, 2M in a case.

.38 WINCHESTER AND MARLIN C. F. SHOT (.38.40)

Adapted to Winchester, Marlin and Colt Repeating rifles; Remington and Winchester Single Shot rifles; also Colt and Smith & Wesson revolvers.

Semi-Smokeless powder, per 1,000 .... **$30.00**
    Size of shot, No. 8.
    Packed 20 in a box, 2M in a case.

.44 GAME GETTER SHOT

Adapted to Marble Game Getter and other Smooth Bore rifles and shot guns.

Semi-Smokeless powder, per 1,000 .... **$30.00**
Smokeless powder, per 1,000 .... **36.00**
    Size of shot, No. 8.
    Packed 50 in a box, 2M in a case.
    Also supplied in No. 6 shot.

CENTER FIRE SHOT CARTRIDGES

.44 X-L SHOT

Adapted to X-L and other shot guns.

Semi-Smokeless powder, per 1,000 .... $31.50
Smokeless powder, per 1,000 .... 37.50
    Size of shot, No. 8.
    Packed 50 in a box, 2M in a case.
    Also supplied in No. 6.

.44 WINCHESTER AND MARLIN C. F. SHOT (.44-40)

Adapted to Winchester, Marlin, Colt and other Repeating rifles; Remington, Winchester, and other Single Shot rifles; also Colt, Smith & Wesson, Merwin-Hulbert & Co., Remington and other revolvers.

Semi-Smokeless powder, per 1,000 .... $30.00
Smokeless powder, per 1,000 .... 36.00
    Size of shot, No. 8.
    Packed 50 in a box, 2M in a case.
    Also supplied in No. 6.

.45 AUTO SHOT

Adapted to Thompson Sub-Machine Gun.

Smokeless powder, per 1,000 .... $54.00
    Size of shot, No. 7½ chilled.
    Packed 50 in a box, 2M in a case.

CENTER FIRE SHOT CARTRIDGES

.38-55 WINCHESTER, MARLIN AND SAVAGE SHOT

Adapted to Winchester Model 1894, Marlin Models 1881 and 1893, Savage, and other Repeating rifles; also to Ballard, Remington and Winchester Single Shot rifles.

Semi-Smokeless powder, per 1,000..$68.00
    Size of shot, No. 8.
    Packed 20 in a box, 1M in a case.

.45-70 GOVERNMENT SHOT

Adapted to Winchester and Marlin Repeating; also to Springfield, Remington and other Single Shot rifles.

Semi-Smokeless powder, per 1,000..$71.50
    Size of shot, No. 8.
    Packed 20 in a box, 1M in a case.

CONDENSED PRICE LIST
Peters Rim Fire Cartridges

Semi-Smokeless in Black Ink.   Smokeless in Red Ink.

	No.	Style of Bullet	Telegraphic Code	List per 1000	Weight of Bullet Grains	Quantity in Box	Quantity in Case	Primed Shells per M
.22 B. B. Cap, Round Ball	112	Lead	Scale	$3.50	20	100	10000	$3.25
.22 C. B. Cap, Conical Ball	113	Lead	Labor	4.40	30	100	10000	3.60
.22 C. B. Cap, Conical Ball	114	Lead	Suffer	4.40	30	100	10000	3.60
.22 C. B. Cap, Non-Lubricant †	115	Lead	Stipulate	4.40	30	100	10000	3.60
.22 Short	2201	Lead	Lagoon	5.00	30	50	10000	3.60
.22 Short	2202	Lead	Solder	5.35	30	50	10000	3.60
.22 Short, Non-Lubricant †	2203	Lead	Sneeze	5.35	30	50	10000	3.60
.22 Short, Hollow Point	2205	Lead	Locate	5.50	30	50	10000	3.60
.22 Short, Hollow Point	2206	Lead	Shank	5.75	30	50	10000	3.60
.22 Short, Hollow Point, Non-Lubricant †	2207	Lead	Shuffle	5.75	30	50	10000	3.60
.22 Long	2208	Lead	Lament	6.00	30	50	10000	4.50
.22 Long	2209	Lead	Sing	7.50	30	50	10000	4.50
.22 Long, Non-Lubricant †	2210	Lead	Syndicate	7.50	30	50	10000	4.50

†These Smokeless sizes supplied with Lubricated bullets (Greased) unless Non-Lubricated bullets are specified. "Semi-Smokeless" cartridges are regular and will be sent unless Smokeless are specified.

Peters Rim Fire Cartridges

Semi-Smokeless in Black Ink.   Smokeless in Red Ink.

	No.	Style of Bullet	Tele-graphic Code	List per 1000	Weight of Bullet Grains	Quantity in Box	Quantity in Case	Primed Shells per M
.22 Long, Hollow Point.	2211	Lead	Limit	$6.50	30	50	10000	$4.50
.22 Long, Hollow Point. †	2212	Lead	Shudder	8.00	30	50	10000	4.50
.22 Long, Hollow Point, Non-Lubricant.	2213	Lead	Syntax	8.00	30	50	10000	4.50
.22 Long Rifle (NRA) (250 Yds.)	2221	Lead	Lark	7.00	40	50	10000	4.50
.22 Long Rifle. †	2216	Lead	Steerage	8.75	40	50	10000	4.50
.22 Long Rifle, Non-Lubricant.	2217	Lead	Steeple	8.75	40	50	10000	4.50
.22 Long Rifle, Hollow Point, (NRA) (250 Yds.)	2222	Lead	Lesson	7.60	38	50	10000	4.50
.22 Long Rifle, Hollow Point. †	2219	Lead	Stentor	9.35	38	50	10000	4.50
.22 Long Rifle, Hollow Point, Non-Lubricant.	2220	Lead	Sterling	9.35	38	50	10000	4.50
.22 Tack Hole (Indoor).	2225	Lead	Lake	8.75	40	50	10000	
.22 Tack Hole (Outdoor).	2226	Lead	Land	8.75	40	50	10000	
.22 Extra Long.	2227	Lead	Logic	10.50	40	50	10000	5.40
.22 Winchester, Mod. 1890.	2228	Lead	Lop	10.50	46	50	5000	5.40

†These Smokeless sizes supplied with Lubricated bullets (Greased) unless Non-Lubricated bullets are specified

"Semi-Smokeless" cartridges are regular and will be sent unless Smokeless are specified.

Peters Rim Fire Cartridges

Semi-Smokeless in Black Ink.   Smokeless in Red Ink.

All Packed 50 in a Box	No.	Style of Bullet	Tele-graphic Code	List per 1000	Weight of Bullet Grains	Quantity in Case	Primed Shells per M
.22 Winchester, Mod. 1890............................†	2229	Lead	Shuck	$11.75	46	5000	$5.40
.22 Winchester, Mod. 1890, Non-Lubricant.........	2230	Lead	Siege	11.75	46	5000	5.40
.22 Winchester, Mod. 1890, Hollow Point..........	2231	Lead	Lophine	11.00	44	5000	5.40
.22 Winchester, Mod. 1890, Hollow Point..........	2232	Lead	Signal	12.25	44	5000	5.40
.22 Winchester Automatic...........................	2233	Lead	Sulphone	11.75	45	5000	
.22 Winchester Automatic, Hollow Point...........	2234	Lead	Satiate	12.25	44	5000	
.22 Remington Auto Loading........................	2235	Lead	Snicker	11.75	47	5000	
.22 Remington Auto Loading, H. P.................	2236	Lead	Snug	12.25	45	5000	
.25 Short Stevens...................................	2501	Lead	Loiter	11.75	68	4000	7.20
.25 Stevens and Marlin..............................	2503	Lead	Lofty	16.50	68	2000	9.00
.25 Stevens and Marlin, Hollow Point..............	2504	Lead	Linger	17.00	65	2000	9.00
.32 Extra Short.....................................	3201	Lead	Lustre	11.75	55	5000	5.40
.32 Short..	3202	Lead	Ledger	11.75	82	5000	6.50
.32 Long...	3205	Lead	Lathe	13.50	90	5000	7.20
.38 Short..	3801	Lead	Lyceum	18.75	125	3000	9.00
.41 Short..	4101	Lead	Lyric	17.50	130	3000	8.00
.41 Swiss...*	4102	Lead	Steam	57.00	300	1000	

†Supplied with Lubricated bullets (Greased) unless Non-Lubricated bullets are specified.
*Packed 20 to a box, 1000 in a case.
"Semi-Smokeless" cartridges are regular and will be sent unless Smokeless are specified.

Peters Center Fire Revolver and Rifle Cartridges

Semi-Smokeless in Black Ink. Smokeless in Red Ink.

Primer No.	†Packed 25 in a box. Others Packed 50 in a Box	No.	Style of Bullet	Telegraphic Code	List per 1000	Weight of Bullet Grains	Quantity in Case	Primed Shells per M	Bullets per M
1½	5.5 m/m. Velo-Dog†	2271	M. C.	Sour	$26.25	45	2000	......	$4.50
1	22 Winchester	2272	Lead	Maritime	26.25	46	2000	$16.25	4.50
1	22 Winchester	2273	Lead	Sobriquet	29.75	46	2000	16.25	4.50
1	25-20 Marlin, Winchester	2551	Lead	Meadow	28.00	86	2000	16.25	7.25
1	25-20 Marlin, Winchester	2552	Lead	Sooth	33.25	86	2000	16.25	7.25
1	25-20 Marlin, Winchester	2553	S. P.	Silken	35.00	86	2000	16.25	9.00
1	25-20 Marlin, Winchester	2554	M. C.	Simoon	35.00	86	2000	16.25	9.00
6½	25-20 High Veloc. Exp'g (Win. and Marlin.)	2555	Exp.	Scenic	35.00	60	2000	......	......
6½	25-20 High Veloc. (Win. and Marlin)	2556	S. P.	Sodium	36.75	86	2000	......	......
	25-20 Stevens and Winchester S. Shot	2557	Lead	Mansard	31.50	86	2000	21.50	7.25
1	25-20 Stevens and Winchester S. Shot	2558	Lead	Sallow	36.75	86	2000	21.50	7.25
1	25-20 Stevens and Winchester S. Shot	2559	S. P.	Simper	38.50	86	2000	21.50	9.00
1	25-20 Stevens and Winchester S. Shot	2560	M. C.	Sinew	38.50	86	2000	21.50	9.00
1½	25 Automatic Pistol	2561	S. P.	Simplex	29.00	50	5000	......	......
1½	25 Automatic Pistol	2562	M. C.	Sibilant	29.00	50	5000	......	......
1½	30 Luger Auto. (7.65 M. M.)	3051	S. P.	Suffrage	45.50	93	2000	......	......
1½	30 Luger Auto. (7.65 M. M.)	3052	M. C.	Sulky	45.50	93	2000	......	......

Smokeless Powder Revolver and Rifle Cartridges supplied with Lead Bullets unless otherwise specified.

Peters Center Fire Revolver and Rifle Cartridges

Semi-Smokeless in Black Ink.   Smokeless in Red Ink.

Primer No.	All Packed 50 in a Box	No.	Style of Bullet	Telegraphic Code	List per 1000	Weight of Bullet Grains	Quantity in Case	Primed Shells per M	Bullets per M
1½	.30 Luger Auto. (7.65 m/m)	3053	H. P.	Sustain	$45.50	93	2000		
1½	.32 Short Colt	3251	Lead	Maroon	19.25	82	5000	$10.75	$5.50
1½	.32 Short Colt	3252	Lead	Soprano	21.00	82	5000	10.75	5.50
1½	.32 Long Colt	3253	Lead	Matting	21.00	82	5000	11.75	5.50
1½	.32 Long Colt	3254	Lead	Sorrel	23.50	82	5000	11.75	5.50
1½	.32 Colt, New Police (Police Positive)	3255	Lead	Mandate	21.00	100	5000	11.75	5.50
1½	.32 Colt, New Police (Police Positive)	3256	Lead	Sizzle	23.50	100	5000	11.75	5.50
1½	.32 Colt, New Police, Metal Pt. (Police Positive)	3257	M. P.	Smear	25.50	96	5000	11.75	5.50
1½	.32 Colt, New Police, Mid. Rge. (Police Positive)	3258	Lead	Seed	20.00	100	5000	11.75	5.50
1½	.32 Automatic Pistol	3259	S. P.	Signify	31.50	73	5000		
1½	.32 Automatic Pistol	3260	M. C.	Silence	31.50	73	5000		
1½	.32 Smith & Wesson	3261	Lead	Magic	19.25	86	5000	10.75	5.50
1½	.32 Smith & Wesson	3262	Lead	Spacious	21.00	86	5000	10.75	5.50
1½	.32 Smith & Wesson, Metal Point	3263	M. P.	Smack	22.75	86	5000	10.75	5.50

Smokeless Powder Revolver and Rifle Cartridges supplied with Lead Bullets unless otherwise specified.

Peters Center Fire Revolver and Rifle Cartridges

Semi-Smokeless in Black Ink.   Smokeless in Red Ink.

Primer No.	All Packed 50 in a Box	No.	Style of Bullet	Telegraphic Code	List per 1000	Weight of Bullet Grains	Quantity in Case	Primed Shells per M	Bullets per M
1½	.32 Smith & Wesson	3264	Lead	Mansion	$21.00	98	5000	$12.25	$6.25
1½	.32 Smith & Wesson, Long	3265	Lead	Spatter	23.50	98	5000	12.25	6.25
1½	.32 Smith & Wesson, Long, Metal Point	3266	M. P.	Smart	25.50	98	5000	12.25	
1	.32 Winchester, C. F. (32-20)	3267	Lead	Mallard	28.00	100	2000	16.25	7.25
1	.32 Winchester, C. F. (32-20)	3269	Lead	Spaniard	33.25	100	2000	16.25	7.25
1	.32 Winchester, C. F. (32-20)	3270	S. P.	Sinister	35.00	100	2000	16.25	9.00
1	.32 Winchester, C. F. (32-20)	3271	M. C.	Siphon	35.00	100	2000	16.25	9.00
6½	.32 Winchester, C. F. High Velocity, Exp (32-20)	3272	Exp.	Scorch	35.00	80	2000		
6½	.32 Winchester, C. F. High Velocity (32-20)	3273	S. P.	Solace	36.75	100	2000		
1	9 m/m Luger	3651	M. C.	Score	47.25	125	2000		
1	9 m/m Luger	3652	H. P.	Scow	47.25	125	2000		
1½	.35 Smith & Wesson Automatic	3571	S. P.	Scintillate	31.50	76	5000		
1½	.35 Smith & Wesson Automatic, Metal Point	3572	M. P.	Scientist	31.50	76	5000		
1½	.38 Smith & Wesson	3821	Lead	Mallet	23.50	146	2000	13.50	8.00

Smokeless Powder Revolver and Rifle Cartridges supplied with Lead Bullets unless otherwise specified.

Peters Center Fire Revolver and Rifle Cartridges

Semi-Smokeless in Black Ink.   Smokeless in Red Ink.

Primer No.	All Packed 50 in a Box	No.	Style of Bullet	Telegraphic Code	List per 1000	Weight of Bullet Grains	Quantity in Case	Primed Shells per M	Bullets per M
1½	.38 Smith & Wesson	3822	Lead	Speller	$27.25	146	2000	$13.50	$8.00
1½	.38 Smith & Wesson, Metal Point	3823	M. P.	Smilax	29.00	146	2000	13.50	
1½	.38 Smith & Wesson Special	3824	Lead	Music	29.00	158	2000	16.25	8.50
1½	.38 Smith & Wesson Special	3825	Lead	Simplify	32.50	158	2000	16.25	8.50
1½	.38 Smith & Wesson Special, Metal Point	3826	M. P.	Smither	34.00	158	2000	16.25	
1½	.38 S. & W. Special "Wad Cutter" Bullet	3827	Lead	Suavity	32.50	147	2000	16.25	8.00
1½	.38 S. & W. Sp'l Mid-R'ge "Wad Cutter" Bullet	3828	Lead	Subdue	28.00	147	2000	16.25	8.00
1½	.38 Smith & Wesson Special Gallery	3829	Lead	Massive	25.50	115	2000	16.25	7.25
1½	.38 Colt New Police (Police Positive)	3830	Lead	Minimize	23.50	150	2000	13.50	8.00
1½	.38 Colt New Police (Police Positive)	3831	Lead	Smuggle	27.25	150	2000	13.50	8.00
1½	.38 Short Colt	3832	Lead	Memory	23.50	125	4000	12.75	7.25
1½	.38 Short Colt	3833	Lead	Squadron	27.25	125	4000	12.75	7.25
1½	.38 Long Colt, D. A.	3834	Lead	Melt	25.50	150	3000	13.50	8.00

Smokeless Powder Revolver and Rifle Cartridges supplied with Lead Bullets unless otherwise specified.

Peters Center Fire Revolver and Rifle Cartridges

Semi-Smokeless in Black Ink.   Smokeless in Red Ink.

All Packed 50 in a Box	Primer No.	No.	Style of Bullet	Telegraphic Code	List per 1000	Weight of Bullet Grains	Quantity in Case	Primed Shells per M	Bullets per M
.38 Long Colt, D. A.	1½	3835	Lead	Stable	$29.00	150	3000	$13.50	$8.00
.38 Long Colt, Metal Point	1½	3836	M.P.	Smudge	30.75	148	3000	13.50	......
.38 Long Colt, D. A., Mid-Range	1½	3837	Lead	Scene	24.50	150	3000	13.50	8.00
.38 Colt Special	1½	3838	Lead	Massacre	29.00	158	2000	16.25	8.50
.38 Colt Special	1½	3839	Lead	Smirk	32.50	158	2000	16.25	8.50
.38 Automatic Pistol	1½	3850	S.P.	Sulphate	45.50	130	2000	......	......
.38 Automatic Pistol	1½	3851	M.C.	Sultan	45.50	130	2000	......	......
.380 Automatic Pistol	1½	3852	S.P.	Secular	43.75	95	2000	......	......
.380 Automatic Pistol	1½	3853	M.C.	Segregate	43.75	95	2000	......	......
.38 Winchester, C. F. (38-40)	1	3854	Lead	Moose	33.25	180	2000	18.00	9.00
.38 Winchester, C. F. (38-40)	1	3856	S.P.	Slogan	42.00	180	2000	18.00	10.75
.38 Winchester, C. F. (38-40)	1	3857	M.C.	Slope	42.00	180	2000	18.00	10.75
.38 Winchester, C. F., High Velocity (38-40)	6½	3858	S.P.	Slave	47.25	180	2000	......	......
.41 Short Colt, D. A.	1½	4151	Lead	Muscle	26.25	160	2000	13.50	7.25

Smokeless Powder Revolver and Rifle Cartridges supplied with Lead Bullets unless otherwise specified.

Peters Center Fire Revolver and Rifle Cartridges

Semi-Smokeless in Black Ink.   Smokeless in Red Ink.

Primer No.	All Packed 50 in a Box	No.	Style of Bullet	Telegraphic Code	List per 1000	Weight of Bullet Grains	Quantity in Case	Primed Shells per M	Bullets per M
1½	.41 Short Colt, D. A.	4152	Lead	Stalwart	$29.75	160	2000	$13.50	$7.25
1½	.41 Long Colt, D. A.	4153	Lead	Mouse	30.75	195	2000	14.50	10.75
1½	.41 Long Colt, D. A.	4154	Lead	Star	35.00	195	2000	14.50	10.75
2X	.44 Smith & Wesson American	4401	Lead	Miracle	33.25	205	2000	15.25	10.75
2X	.44 Smith & Wesson Russian Model	4402	Lead	Master	35.00	246	2000	17.00	11.75
2X	.44 Smith & Wesson Russian Model	4403	Lead	Sandal	38.50	246	2000	17.00	11.75
2X	.44 Smith & Wesson Special	4404	Lead	Minikin	38.50	246	2000	19.75	11.75
2X	.44 Smith & Wesson Special	4405	Lead	Surcease	42.00	246	2000	19.75	11 75
2X	.44 Smith & Wesson Special, Metal Point	4406	M. P.	Smut	43.75	246	2000	19.75	
1	.44 Winchester, C. F. (.44-40)	4407	Lead	Mount	33.25	200	2000	18.00	10.75
1	.44 Winchester, C. F. (.44-40)	4409	S. P.	Slouch	42.00	200	2000	18.00	12.50
1	.44 Winchester, C. F. (.44-40)	4410	M. C.	Sluice	42.00	200	2000	18.00	12.50
1	.44 Winchester, C. F., Hollow Point (.44-40)	4411	Lead	Moonlight	34.00	165	2000	18.00	11.75

Smokeless Powder Revolver and Rifle Cartridges supplied with Lead Bullets unless otherwise specified.

Peters Center Fire Revolver and Rifle Cartridges

Semi-Smokeless in Black Ink. **Smokeless in Red Ink.**

Primer No.	All Packed 50 in a Box	No.	Style of Bullet	Telegraphic Code	List per 1000	Weight of Bullet Grains	Quantity in Case	Primed Shells per M	Bullets per M
6½	.44 Winchester, C. F., High Velocity (.44-40)..	4413	S. P.	Sluggish	$47.25	200	2000		
2X	.44 Webley	4414	Lead	Magenta	29.00	200	2000	$14.50	$10.75
2X	.44 Bull Dog	4415	Lead	Magnesia	25.50	168	2000	13.50	9.00
1	.44 Game Getter	4416	Lead	Mortal	33.25	119	2000	18.00	
1	.44 Game Getter	4417	Lead	Steward	38.50	119	2000	18.00	
2X	.45 Colt U. S. A.	4501	Lead	Mogul	38.50	255	2000	19.00	12.50
2X	.45 Colt U. S. A.	4502	Lead	Sergeant	43.00	255	2000	19.00	12.50
2X	.45 Colt Automatic	4503	M. C.	Sombre	52.50	200	2000		
2X	.45 Colt Automatic, Government Model	4504	M. C.	Sovereign	52.50	230	2000		
2X	.45 Auto Rim*	4505	M. C.	Solicit	52.50	230	2000		
2X	.45 Auto Rim*	4506	Lead	Soak	51.00	255	2000		

*Use instead of automatic cartridge with clips.

Smokeless Powder Revolver and Rifle Cartridges supplied with Lead Bullets unless otherwise specified.

Peters Center Fire Military and Sporting Cartridges

Semi-Smokeless in Black Ink.   Smokeless in Red Ink.

Packed 20 in a box, 1000 in a case

Primer No.		No.	Style of Bullet	Telegraphic Code	List per 1000	Weight of Bullet Grains	Primed Shells per M	Bullets per M
11	7 m/m Mauser	2801	S. P.	Uranyl	$95.00	175	$36.00	$27.00
11	7 m/m Mauser	2802	M. C.	Uncilia	95.00	175	36.00	27.00
11	7.65 m/m Mauser	3061	S. P.	Undaunted	95.00	219	36.00	27.00
11	7.65 m/m Mauser	3062	M. C.	Undimmed	95.00	219	36.00	27.00
11	.22 Savage High Power	2261	S. P.	Unbidden	72.25	70	27.00	9.00
11	.22 Savage High Power	2262	M. C.	Unblown	72.25	70	27.00	9.00
11½	.250 Savage High Power	2571	PP Exp	Unheard	82.00	87	38.50	29.00
11½	.250 Savage High Power	2572	S. P.	Unjust	80.00	87	38.50	27.00
11½	.250 Savage High Power	2573	M. C.	Ugly	80.00	87	38.50	27.00
11	.25-35 Savage and Winchester (High Velocity)	2574	S. P.	Upset	62.75	117	27.00	9.00
11	.25-35 Savage and Winchester (High Velocity)	2575	M. C.	Uprouse	62.75	117	27.00	9.00
11	.25-36 Marlin	2576	S. P.	Upper	62.75	117	27.00	9.00
11½	.25 Remington Auto. (Rimless) (High Velocity)	2577	S. P.	Umbrade	62.75	117		
11½	.25 Remington Auto. (Rimless) (High Velocity)	2578	M. C.	Ulnage	62.75	117		
11	.270 Winchester	2701	PP Exp	Utrex	106.50	130	40.50	29.00
11	.30-30 Marlin, Winchester, Savage (High Velocity)	3063	S. P.	Unloose	72.25	170	32.50	10.75
11	.30-30 Marlin, Winchester, Savage (M. C. H. P. Exp.)	3093	HP Exp	Unyoke	72.25	125		
11	.30-30 Marlin, Winchester, Savage (M. C. H. P. Exp.)	3092	HP Exp	Usury	72.25	165		

Cartridges supplied with Soft Point Bullets unless otherwise specified.

Peters Center Fire Military and Sporting Cartridges

Semi-Smokeless in Black Ink. Smokeless in Red Ink.

Primer No.	Packed 20 in a box, 1000 in a case	No.	Style of Bullet	Telegraphic Code	List per 1000	Weight of Bullet Grains	Primed Shells per M	Bullets per M
11	.30-30 Marlin, Winchester, Savage (High Velocity)...	3064	M. C.	Universe	$72.25	160	$32.50	$10.75
11	.30 Remington	3065	S. P.	Ufanar	72.25	170	......	......
11	.30 Remington	3066	M. C.	Ubicos	72.25	160	......	......
11	.30 Remington (M. C. Hollow Point Exp.)...	3095	HP Exp	Umbra	72.25	125	......	......
11	.30 Remington (M. C. Hollow Point Exp.)...	3094	HP Exp	Ukase	72.25	165	......	......
11	.30-40 U. S. Army (Krag)	3067	S. P.	Unfasten	95.00	220	36.00	27.00
11	.30-40 U. S. Army (Krag)	3068	M. C.	Upturn	95.00	220	36.00	27.00
11	.30-40-150 Krag Sharp Pointed Bullet	3069	S. P.	Uncivil	95.00	150	36.00	27.00
11	.30-40-150 (Krag)	3070	PP. Exp	Undefiled	97.00	150	36.00	29.00
11	.30-40-180 (Krag) Sharp Pointed Bullet	3071	S. P.	Unanimous	95.00	180	36.00	27.00
11	.30-40-180 (Krag)	3072	PP. Exp	Unruly	97.00	180	36.00	29.00
11	.30 Government, 1903	3073	S. P.	Ulluco	104.50	220	40.50	27.00
11	.30 Government, 1903	3074	M. C.	Ulmaceous	104.50	220	40.50	27.00
11	.30 Government, 1906, Sharp Pointed Bullet	3075	S. P.	Uplift	104.50	150	40.50	27.00
11	.30 Government, 1906, Sharp Pointed Bullet	3076	M. C.	Ugrian	104.50	150	40.50	27.00
11	.30 Government, 1906	3077	PP. Exp	Ultimo	106.50	150	40.50	29.00
11	.30 Government, 1906, Sharp Pointed Bullet	3078	S. P.	Ulcer	104.50	180	40.50	27.00
11	.30 Government, 1906, Sharp Pointed Bullet	3079	M. C.	Ubiety	104.50	180	40.50	27.00
11	.30 Government, 1906	3080	PP. Exp	Upstart	106.50	180	40.50	29.00

Cartridges supplied with Soft Point Bullets unless otherwise specified.

Peters Center Fire Military and Sporting Cartridges

Semi-Smokeless in Black Ink.   **Smokeless in Red Ink.**

Packed 20 in a box, 1000 in a case

Primer No.		No.	Style of Bullet	Telegraphic Code	List per 1000	Weight of Bullet Grains	Primed Shells per M	Bullets per M
11	30 Government, 1906, Round Nose	3081	S. P.	Unit	$104.50	220	$40.50	$27.00
11½	300 Caliber Savage	3084	PP Exp	Unseal	92.00	150	38.50	29.00
11	303 British	3085	S. P.	Uratic	95.00	215	36.00	27.00
11	303 British	3086	M. C.	Uralite	95.00	215	36.00	27.00
11	303 Savage	3088	S. P.	Uproot	72.25	190	33.25	19.00
11	303 Savage	3089	M. C.	Unhorse	72.25	190	33.25	19.00
11	8 m/m Mauser (7.9 m/m)	3101	S. P.	Ulterior	95.00	170	36.00	27.00
11	8 m/m Mauser (7.9 m/m)	3102	M. C.	Unsightly	95.00	227	36.00	27.00
11	8 m/m Mannlicher-Sch. Model 1908	3103	S. P.	Urban	95.00	200	36.00	27.00
11	8 m/m Mannlicher-Sch. Model 1908	3104	M. C.	Urao	95.00	227	36.00	27.00
11	.32 Winchester Special	3281	S. P.	Unmast	72.25	165	32.50	14.75
11	.32 Winchester Special	3282	M. C.	Uncertain	72.25	165	32.50	14.75
6½	.32 Winchester, Self-Loading †	3283	S. P.	Uberous	51.25	165		
6½	.32 Winchester, Self-Loading †	3284	M. C.	Ursiform	51.25	165		
11½	.32 Remington Auto. (Rimless)	3285	S. P.	Urticate	72.25	165		
11½	.32 Remington Auto. (Rimless)	3286	M. C.	Utraquist	72.25	165		
11	32-40 Winchester, Marlin and Savage	3287	Lead	Ultra	51.25	165	27.00	13.00

Smokeless Powder Military and Sporting Cartridges supplied with Soft Point Bullets unless otherwise specified.
†Packed 50 in a box, 2000 in a case.

Peters Center Fire Military and Sporting Cartridges

Semi-Smokeless in Black Ink.   Smokeless in Red Ink.

Primer No.	Packed 20 in a box, 1000 in a case	No.	Style of Bullet	Telegraphic Code	List per 1000	Weight of Bullet Grains	Primed Shells per M	Bullets per M
11	32-40 Winchester, Marlin and Savage	3288	S. P.	Unify	$60.75	165	$27.00	$14.75
11	32-40 Winchester, Marlin and Savage	3289	M. C.	Unison	60.75	165	27.00	14.75
11	32-40 High Velocity	3290	S. P.	Uncouple	72.25	165	32.50	14.75
11	33 Winchester	3391	S. P.	Urtical	95.00	200	46.75	19.00
11	35 Winchester	3591	S. P.	Usbecks	104.50	250	36.00	21.50
6½	35 Winchester, Self-Loading	3581	S. P.	Udalman	52.25	180		
6½	35 Winchester, Self-Loading	3582	M. C.	Urgency	52.25	180		
11½	35 Remington Auto. (Rimless)	3583	S. P.	Ulema	79.75	200		
11½	35 Remington Auto. (Rimless) †	3584	M. C.	Umbellule	79.75	200		
6½	351 Winchester, Self-Loading	3585	S. P.	Uncial	60.75	180		
6½	351 Winchester, Self-Loading †	3586	M. C.	Undercut	60.75	180		
11	38-55 Winchester, Marlin and Savage	3871	Lead	Until	62.75	255	32.50	17.00
11	38-55 Winchester, Marlin and Savage	3872	S. P.	Unique	76.00	255	32.50	19.00
11	38-55 Winchester, Marlin and Savage	3873	M. C.	Unitary	76.00	255	32.50	19.00
11	38-55 Winchester, Marlin and Savage, High Velocity	3874	S. P.	Unjoint	87.50	255	37.75	19.00
11	38-56 Winchester and Marlin	3875	Lead	Umpire	62.75	255	32.50	17.00

Smokeless Powder Military and Sporting Cartridges supplied with Soft Point Bullets unless otherwise specified.
†Packed 50 in a box, 2000 in a case.

Peters Center Fire Military and Sporting Cartridges

Semi-Smokeless in Black Ink.   Smokeless in Red Ink.

Primer No.	Packed 20 in a box, 1000 in a case	No.	Style of Bullet	Telegraphic Code	List per 1000	Weight of Bullet Grains	Primed Shells per M	Bullets per M
11	38-56 Winchester and Marlin	3876	S. P.	Unkempt	$76.00	255	$32.50	$19.00
11	40-65 Winchester and Marlin	4051	Lead	Umbrella	62.75	260	32.50	16.25
11	40-65 Winchester and Marlin	4052	S. P.	Unlatch	76.00	260	32.50	18.00
11	40-82 Winchester and Marlin	4053	Lead	Ultimate	68.50	260	43.25	16.25
11	40-82 Winchester and Marlin	4054	S. P.	Unlimber	81.75	260	43.25	18.00
11	401 Winchester, Self-Loading	4061	S. P.	Ultion	76.00	200		
11	401 Winchester, Self-Loading	4062	M. C.	Umbo	76.00	200		
11	401 Winchester, Self-Loading	4063	S. P.	Umhofo	76.00	250		
11	405 Winchester	4071	S. P.	Ustulate	114.00	300	48.50	27.00
11	405 Winchester	4072	M. C.	Uvitic	114.00	300	48.50	27.00
11	45-60 Winchester	4551	Lead	Utter	62.75	300	36.00	16.25
11	45-70 Government	4552	Lead	Unbolt	66.50	405	39.50	21.50
11	45-70 Government	4553	S. P.	Upbraid	79.75	405	39.50	23.50
11	45-70 Government	4554	M. C.	Upcast	79.75	405	39.50	23.50
11	45-90 Winchester and Marlin	4555	Lead	Unbutton	68.50	300	43.25	16.25
11	45-90 Winchester and Marlin	4556	S. P.	Usher	81.75	300	43.25	18.00

Smokeless Powder Military and Sporting Cartridges supplied with Soft Point Bullets unless otherwise specified.

Peters Blank Cartridges

Black Powder in Black Ink.   **Smokeless in Red Ink.**
Loaded with a special powder insuring cleanliness and loud report.

RIM FIRE

	No.	Telegraphic Code	List per 1000	Quantity in Box	Quantity in Case
.22 Short....................	2249	Terror	$ 3.00	50	10000
.32 Short....................	3209	Tenor	5.50	50	5000

CENTRAL FIRE—REVOLVER SIZES

	No.	Telegraphic Code	List per 1000	Quantity in Box	Quantity in Case
.32 Short Colt...............	3296	Tegument	$17.25	50	5000
.32 Smith & Wesson...........	3297	Tenant	11.00	50	5000
.38 Smith & Wesson...........	3894	Tulle	14.00	50	2000
.38 Short Colt...............	3896	Telltale	20.00	50	4000
.38 Long Colt................	3897	Tuxtle	22.75	50	3000
.44 Winchester (44-40).......	4498	Tension	30.00	50	2000
.44 Webley...................	4499	Tendency	26.00	50	2000
.45 Colt.....................	4593	Termagant	34.75	50	2000

CENTRAL FIRE—MILITARY AND SPORTING SIZES

	No.	Telegraphic Code	List per 1000	Quantity in Box	Quantity in Case
.30-40........................	3091	Turmoil	85.50	20	1000
.30 Government, 1906..........	3096	Tussle	94.00	20	1000
.45-70........................	4594	Twig	60.00	20	1000

All other blank cartridges take same list as ball cartridges.

Peters Shot Cartridges

Semi-Smokeless in Black Ink.   Smokeless in Red Ink.

RIM FIRE

	Size of Shot	No.	Telegraphic Code	List per 1000	Quantity in Case
B. B.	12	118	Think	$ 8.00	10000
.22 Long	11	2248	Thine	11.00	10000
.22 Long	11	2249	Thing	12.50	10000
.32 Long	10	3208	Thick	22.00	5000
.41 Swiss	8	4118	Thistle	57.00	1000

CENTRAL FIRE—REVOLVER AND RIFLE SIZES

	Size of Shot	No.	Telegraphic Code	List per 1000	Quantity in Case
.32 Smith & Wesson	10	3293	Theory	18.00	5000
.32 Winchester, C. F. (.32-20)	9	3294	Twinkle	25.50	2000
.38 Smith & Wesson	8	3891	Theme	21.75	2000
.38 Winchester, C. F. (.38-40)	8	3892	Turnip	30.00	2000
.44 Game Getter	6x	4482	Tussock	30.00	2000
.44 Game Getter	6x	4483	Turbid	36.00	2000
.44 Game Getter	8x	4484	Trick	30.00	2000
.44 Game Getter	8x	4485	Trim	36.00	2000
.44 X. L.	6x	4486	Twirl	31.50	2000
.44 X. L.	6x	4487	Twister	37.50	2000
.44 X. L.	8x	4488	Troll	31.50	2000
.44 X. L.	8x	4489	Tripod	37.50	2000
.44 Winchester, C. F. (.44-40)	6x	4490	Turbine	30.00	2000
.44 Winchester, C. F. (.44-40)	8x	4491	Thatch	30.00	2000
.44 Winchester, C. F. (.44-40)	6x	4492	Tense	36.00	2000
.44 Winchester, C. F. (.44-40)	8x	4493	Turquoise	36.00	2000
.45 Auto. (for Thompson Sub-Machine Gun)	7½ Ch.	4525	Thug	54.00	2000

CENTRAL FIRE—MILITARY AND SPORTING SIZES

All packed 20 in a box, 1000 in a case

	Size of Shot	No.	Telegraphic Code	List per 1000
.38-55 Winchester, Marlin and Savage	8	3895	Trinket	$68.00
.45-70 Government	8	4595	Tremble	71.50

x On unspecified orders will send No. 8 Shot.

80

CARTRIDGES IN GROUPS BELOW WILL INTERCHANGE

RIM FIRE

.22 W. R. F.	.25 Stevens Short
.22 Remington Special	.25 Stevens
.22 Winchester Mod. 1890	
.32 Short	.38 Short
.32 Long	.38 Long

CENTER FIRE

.25/20 Win.-Mar.-Rem.	.30/30 Win.-Mar.-Sav. (High Vel.)
.25/20 Win. & Mar.	.30/30 Win.-Mar.-Sav.
.25/20 W. C. F.	.30/30 Winchester
.25/20 Winchester	.30/30 Marlin
.25/20 Marlin	.30 W. C. F.
.25/20 High Velocity, Exp.*	.30/30 M. C. Exp. Hol. Pt.
	8 m/m Mauser
.32 Short Colt	8 m/m Mannlicher
.32 Long Colt	7.9 m/m Mauser
	.25 Colt Automatic
.32 S. & W.	.25 Automatic Pistol
.32 S. & W. Gallery	.25 (6.35 m/m) Auto Pistol
	6.35 Browning Auto
.32 Win.-Mar.-Rem.	.32 Colt Automatic
.32 Win. & Marlin	.32 Automatic Pistol
.32 W. C. F.	.32 (7.65 m/m) Auto Pistol
.32 Winchester	7.65 m/m Auto Pistol
.32/20 Marlin	
.32/20 Colt L. M. R.	.32 S. & W. Long
.32/20 W. C. F.	.32 Colt's New Police
.32/20 Win. & Mar.	.32 Colt's Police Positive
.32/20 High Velocity, Exp.*	
	.38 Short Colt
.38 S. & W.	.38 Long Colt
.38 Colt New Police (Positive)	.38 Long Colt, Mid-Range
	.38 Colt Special
.38 Win.-Mar.-Rem.	.38 S. & W. Special
.38 Winchester	.38 S. & W. Special Wad-Cutter
.38 Remington	
.38/40 Win.	.44 Win.-Mar.-Rem.
.38 W. C. F.	.44 Winchester
	.44 Remington
	.44/40 Win.
.25 Rem. Auto	.44 W. C. F.
.25 Rem. Auto (High Velocity)	
	.45/70 Gov't.
.25/35 Sav. and Win.	.45/70 Gov't. Flat
.25/35 Sav. and Win. (High Vel.)	.45/70 Marlin
	.45/70/405
.30 Rem. Rimless	.45/70/500
.30 Rem. Rimless M.C. Exp. Hol. Pt.	.45/70 High Velocity

*High Velocity (or High Power) Cartridges should not be used in Revolvers, nor in any guns except those made specially for them.

Bullets shown as metal point have lead bearing on the barrel; are metal case on point only.

.22 Smokeless Lubricated (Greased) Cartridges sent on unspecified orders.

PROTECTED POINT EXPANDING cartridges are interchangeable with corresponding cartridges with soft point bullets.

Average Ballistics of Popular Peters Cartridges

RIM FIRE CARTRIDGES—RIFLE BALLISTICS

	Bullet Weight Gr.	Velocities Feet per Sec.		Energies Foot Pounds		Trajectory—Inches Height at Mid-Range				Range of Accuracy in Yds.	Penetration in 7/8" Pine Boards Lead
		Muzzle	100 Yds.	Muzzle	100 Yds.	100 Yds.	200 Yds.	300 Yds.			
.22 Short...............	30	920	778	56.4	40.3	6.1	28.8	78.3		25– 50	....
.22 Short, Smo........	30	903	764	54.3	38.9	6.2	30.5	81.6		25– 50	....
.22 Long...............	30	1030	859	69.0	48.0	4.9	20.8	63.4		50–100	....
.22 Long, Smo.........	30	950	801	58.7	41.7	5.9	25.3	73.5		50–100	....
.22 Long Rifle (NRA)..	40	1055	915	99.3	74.4	4.5	20.7	53.1		100–200	6
.22 Long Rifle Tack-Hole Indoor..	40	930	819	76.8	59.6	5.7	24.5	60.5		50	5
.22 Long Rifle Tack-Hole Outdoor...	40	1065	922	100.8	75.5	4.4	20.6	52.5		100–250	6
.22 Long Rifle, Smo...	40	930	819	76.8	59.6	5.7	24.5	60.5		100–200	5
.22 Extra Long.........	40	1050	911	97.9	72.0	4.6	20.9	53.6		100–200	6
.22 Winchester.........	46	1135	934	128.8	87.2	4.1	19.7	52.4		100–200	7
.22 Winchester, Smo...	45	1065	894	113.3	79.9	4.6	21.8	57.0		100–200	6
.22 Winchester Auto. Smo..	45	1050	885	110.2	78.3	4.7	21.9	57.4		50–100	6
.22 Remington Auto. Smo..	47	1050	885	110.2	78.3	4.7	21.9	57.4		50–100	6
.25 Stevens.............	68	1100	993	182.8	145.5	4.0	17.6	43.4		100–200	7

NOTE—Cartridges loaded with Semi-Smokeless Powder, unless otherwise noted. Trajectories shown are the height at mid-range over the ranges shown. Velocities are given in feet per second; Energies in foot pounds.

Average Ballistics of Popular Peters Cartridges

CENTER FIRE CARTRIDGES—REVOLVER AND PISTOL BALLISTICS

	Barrel Length Inches	Bullet Weight Gr.	Velocities Feet Per Second		Energies Foot Pounds	
			Muzzle	100 Yds.	Muzzle	100 Yds
.25 A. C. P., Smo. S. P. and M. C.	2	50	745	650	61.6	46.0
.30 Luger Smo., S. P. and M. C. (7.65 m/m)	4½	93	1173	1031	284.	174.4
.32 Short Colt and Smo.	6	82	680	611	82.3	68.7
.32 Long Colt.	6	82	690	610	86.6	67.6
.32 Long Colt, Smo.	6	82	720	636	94.4	72.6
.32 Colt, N. P. and Smo.	4	100	730	660	117.	96.7
.32 A. C. P., Smo., S. P. and M. C. (7.65 Br.)	3¾	73	965	847	151.	113.
.32 S. & W., Smo.	4¼	85	635	560	76.	59.2
.32 S. & W. Long and Smo.	4¼	98	720	650	112.7	92.6
.32/20 and Smo. Lead, S. P. and M. C.	6	100	954	874	232.	169.4
9 m/m Luger Smo. M. C. and H. P.	4	125	1040	930	300.	2.40
.35 S. & W. Auto. Smo., S. P. and M. P.	3½	76	809		111.	
.38 S. & W. and Smo.	4	146	632	574	132.4	106.8
.38 S. & W. Special and Smo.	6	158	860	798	258.	218.4
.38 S. & W. Special Mid-Range Wad-Cutter	6	147	675			

Average Ballistics of Popular Peters Cartridges
CENTER FIRE CARTRIDGES—REVOLVER AND PISTOL BALLISTICS

	Barrel Length Inches	Bullet Weight Gr.	Velocities Feet Per Second		Energies Foot Pounds	
			Muzzle	100 Yds.	Muzzle	100 Yds.
.38 Colt N. P. and Smo.	4¼	150	610	556	124.	103.
.38 Short Colt and Smo.	6	125	630	563	107.	88.
.38 Long Colt and Smo.	6	150	800	735	213.	180.
.38 Long Colt D. A. Mid-Range	6	150	660		145.	
.38 A. C. P. Smo., S. P. and M. C.	6	130	1190	1026	408.	303.
.380 A. C. P. Smo., S. P. and M. C.	3¾	95	900	789	171.	131.
.38 Colt Special	6	158	860	798	258.	218.4
.38 Win. (.38/40) Smo., S. P. and M. C.	5½	180	985.8	867	389.	300.
.41 Short Colt and Smo.	6	160	710	636	179.	143.7
.41 Long Colt and Smo.	6	196	715	654	222.	186.
.44 S. & W. American	6	205	682	625	212.	177.
.44 S. & W. Russian	6	246	712	659	277.	237.
.44 S. & W. Special	6	246	780	724	332.	286.
.44 Win. (.44/40) Smo., S. P. and M. C.	5½	200	918.8	808	375.	290.
.45 Colt	5½	255	790	729	353.	301.
.45 A. C. P., M. C., Smo., 200 Gr.	5	200	910	847	368.	319.
.45 A. C. P., M. C., Smo., 230 Gr.	5	230	809	761	335.	295.8
.45 Auto. Rim, M. C., Smo., 230 Gr.	5½	230	809	761	335.	295.8
.45 Auto. Rim Lead, Smo.	5½	255	740	682	310.	263.4

Average Ballistics of Popular Peters Cartridges

CENTER FIRE CARTRIDGES—RIFLE BALLISTICS

Cartridge	Bullet W'ght Gr.	Velocities Feet Per Second Muzzle	Velocities Feet Per Second 100 Yds.	Energies Foot Pounds Muzzle	Energies Foot Pounds 100 Yds.	Trajectory 100 Yds.	Trajectory 200 Yds.	Trajectory 300 Yds.	Range of Accuracy in Yards	Penetration Lead	Penetration S.P.	Penetration M.C.	Penetration H.P. or Exp.
.22 Win. Sing. Shot	46	1565	1137	250	132.1	2.5	13.0	38.1	100–200	8			
.25/20	86	1380	1112	363	236	2.9	14.1	41.0	100–200	9			
.25/20 Smo., Lead, S. P. and M. C.	86	1380	1112	363	236	2.9	14.1	41.0	100–200	9	8	12	
.25/20 H. V. Smo., S. P.	86	1730	1408	571	379	1.9	8.9	24.3	100		10		
.25/20 H. V. Smo., 60 G., Exp. Bullet	60	2200	1604	645	342	1.3	8.2	27.0	200–300				8
.25/20 Single Shot	86	1470	1254	413	298	2.4	12.4	32.5	100–200	9			
.25/20 Sing. Shot, Smo., Lead, S. P. and M. C.	86	1470	1254	413	298	2.4	12.4	32.5	100–200	9	8	12	
.32/20 Lead and Smo., S. P. and M. C.	100	1325	1060	390	249	2.2	15.4	41.0	150–200	6½	6½	11	
.32/20 H. V., Smo., S. P.	100	1640	1224	598	333	2.1	11.4	30.8	100		10		
.32/20 H. V., Smo., 80 Gr., Exp. Bullet	80	2000	1523	710	412	1.4	7.6	25.0	200–300				9
.38/40 S. P. and M. C., Lead and Smo.	180	1325	1054	701	444	3.2	15.5	41.6	150–200	8	10	12	
.38/40 H. V., Smo., S. P.	180	1770	1390	1253	772	1.8	9.3	25.6	100		8		
.44/40 Lead and Smo., S. P. and M. C.	200	1310	1039	752	478	3.3	16.0	42.4	150–200	9	10	13	
.44/40 H. V., Smo., S. P.	200	1565	1226	1086	668	2.3	11.6	31.2	100		10		
7 m/m Mauser Smokl., S. P. and M. C.	175	2300	2052	2056	1923	.91	5.41	10.9	800–1000		12	60	
7.65 m/m Mauser Smo., S. P. and M. C.	219	2030	1850	2004	1665	1.09	5.44	13.96	800–1000		12	56	
8 m/m Mauser, Smo., M. C.	227	2050	1840	2130	1704	1.2	5.9	14.2	800–1000			54	
8 m/m Mauser, Smo., S. P.	170	2500	2222	2360	1863	.75	3.5	11.6	500–700		13		
8m/m Mannlicher-Schoenauer Smo., S.P.	200	2105	1837	1965	1498	.97	4.9	12.1	800–1000		12		
8m/m Mannlicher-Schoenauer Smo., M.C	227	2050	1840	2130	1704	1.2	5.9	14.2	800–1000			54	
.22 Sav. H. P. Smo., S. P. and M. C.	70	2800	2451	1218	917	.63	2.96	7.75	300–500		12	52	

Average Ballistics of Popular Peters Cartridges
CENTER FIRE CARTRIDGES—RIFLE BALLISTICS

	Bullet W'ght Gr.	Velocities Feet Per Second			Energies Foot Pounds			Trajectory, Inches Height at Mid-Range				Range of Accuracy in Yards	Penetration in 7/8" Pine Boards			
		Muzzle	100 Yds.		Muzzle	100 Yds.		100 Yds.	200 Yds.	300 Yds.			Lead	S.P.	M.C.	H.P. or Exp.
.250/3000 Sav. H. P. Smo., P. P. Exp., S. P. and M. C.	87	3000	2643		1737	1349		.54	2.49	6.49		500– 700		14	52	12
.25/35 Smo., S.P. and M. C. (H.V.)	117	2115	1828		1162	868		1.12	5.21	13.77		500– 700		11	36	
.25/36 S. P. Smo.	117	1860	1577		899	645		1.44	7.38	18.90		500– 700		11		
.25 Rem. Smo., S. P. and M. C. (H.V.)	117	2300	2008		1374	1048		.87	4.36	11.51		500– 700		11	44	
.270 Win. P. P. Exp.	130	3160	2970		2880	2550		.5	2.	4.5		800–1000				
.30/30 Smo., M. C. (High Velocity)	160	2200	1899		1718	1266		1.1	4.9	13.1		500– 700			42	
.30/30 Smo., S. P. (High Velocity)	170	2200	1929		1827	1405		1.02	4.37	12.17		500– 700		11		
.30/30 Smo. M. C. Holl. Point Exp.	125	2550	2194		1803	1334		.77	3.49	9.72		500– 700				14
.30/30 Smo. M. C. Holl. Point Exp.	165	2250	1930		1860	1363		.99	4.68	12.51		500– 700				12
.30 Rem. S. P. Smo	170	2020	1750		1540	1153		1.28	5.74	15.21		500– 700		11		
.30 Rem. M. C., Smo.	160	2020	1727		1450	1060		1.31	5.91	15.61		500– 700			42	
.30 Rem. Smo. M. C. Holl. Point Exp.	125	2450	2101		1664	1227		.84	3.97	10.61		500– 700				14
.30 Rem. Smo. M. C. Holl. Point Exp.	165	2250	1930		1860	1363		.99	4.68	12.51		500– 700				12
.300 Savage, P. P. Exp.	150	2700	2465		2426	2034		.64	2.94	7.28		700– 800				14
.30/40 Smo., S. P. and M. C.	220	2005	1830		1972	1636		1.18	5.41	13.55		800–1000	13	13	58	
.30/40 Smo. 150Gr. Exp. P.P., S.P.&M.C.	150	2560	2327		2183	1804		.79	3.42	9.00		800		16	62	15
.30/40 Smo., 180 Gr., S.P. and P. P. Exp.	180	2350	2187		2208	1912		.84	3.43	8.81		800–1000		16		16
.30 Gov. '03 Smo., S. P. and M. C.	220	2210	2001		2365	1974		.97	4.51	11.41		800–1000		18	68	
.30 Gov. '06 Smo., Exp. P. P., S. P. and M. C. 150 Gr.	150	2700	2465		2429	2034		.64	2.94	7.28		1000–1200		16	75	18
.30 Gov. '06 Smo., Exp. P. P., S. P. and M. C. 180 Gr.	180	2500	2314		2498	2140		.75	3.27	7.94		800–1000		18	68	19
.30 Gov. '06 Smo. S. P. & M. C. 220 Gr.	220	2210	2001		2365	1974		.96	4.51	11.40		1000–1200		18	68	
.303 Sav. Smo., S. P. and M. C.	190	2000	1763		1686	1311		1.23	5.62	14.43		500– 700		11	42	
.303 Brit. Smo., S. P. and M. C.	215	2005	1820		1920	1583		1.26	5.51	14.03		800–1000		13	56	

Average Ballistics of Popular Peters Cartridges
CENTER FIRE CARTRIDGES—RIFLE BALLISTICS

	Bullet W'ght Gr.	Velocities Feet Per Second		Energies Foot Pounds		Trajectory, Inches Height at Mid-Range			Range of Accuracy in Yards	Penetration in ⅞" Pine Boards			
		Muzzle	100 Yds.	Muzzle	100 Yds.	100 Yds.	200 Yds.	300 Yds.		Lead	S.P.	M.C.	H.P. or Exp.
.32 Win. Spl., Smo., S. P. and M. C.	165	2120	1802	1647	1190	1.15	5.62	14.62	500–700	....	12	48	....
.32 Win. S Ldg., Smo., S. P. and M.C.	165	1400	1174	718	658	2.70	12.48	33.25	200–300	....	10	17	....
.32 Rem. Smo., S. P. and M. C.	165	2115	1772	1689	1123	1.15	5.31	14.82	500–700	....	12	46	....
32/40 Semi-Smo	165	1450	1200	770	528	2.39	12.08	31.52	300–500	9	....	....	....
32/40 Smo., S. P. and M. C.	165	1505	1249	830	572	2.31	10.86	29.28	300–500	....	9	18	....
32/40 H. V., Smo., S. P.	165	2065	1708	1558	1072	1.22	5.47	15.64	500–700	....	10	....	....
.33 Win., Smo., S. P.	200	2060	1762	1885	1379	1.20	5.64	14.95	500–700	....	14	....	....
.35 Win., Smo., S. P.	250	2200	1952	2687	2116	1.03	4.61	11.82	500–700	....	15	....	....
.35 Win. S Ldg., Smo., S. P. and M. C.	180	1455	1175	846	552	2.65	12.75	34.31	200–300	....	9	17	....
.35 Rem., Auto. Smo., S. P. and M. C.	200	2020	1697	1811	1279	1.27	5.93	16.17	500–700	....	13	32	....
.351 Win., S. Ldg., Smo., S. P. and M. C	180	1875	1562	1405	975	1.16	7.20	19.97	300–500	....	13	28	....
38/55 and Smo., S. P. and M. C.	255	1325	1135	989	582	2.87	13.56	34.42	300–500	10	14	18	....
38/55 H. V., Smo., S. P.	255	1770	1436	1635	1165	1.78	8.19	20.95	500–700	....	11	....	....
38/56 and Smo., S. P. and M. C.	255	1445	1263	1183	901	2.00	11.52	29.16	300–500	11	12	24	....
40/65 and Smo., S. P.	260	1370	1148	1084	761	2.59	13.24	33.42	300–500	9	12	....	....
40/82 and Smo., S. P.	260	1500	1245	1299	895	2.36	11.26	29.88	300–500	12	11	....	....
.401 Win. S Ldg. Smo. S.P.&M.C. 200Gr.	200	2145	1725	2044	1322	1.21	5.76	16.11	300–500	....	14	34	....
.401 Win., S. Ldg., Smo., S. P., 250 Gr.	250	1875	1543	1952	1323	1.49	7.14	20.16	300–500	....	12	....	....
.405 Win., Smo., S. P. and M. C.	300	2210	1903	3254	2413	1.03	4.69	12.21	500–700	....	13	48	....
.45/60	300	1315	1092	1158	794	3.07	14.50	37.35	300–500	12	14	....	....
.45/70/405 and Smo., S. P. and M. C.	405	1350	1168	1649	1227	2.65	11.90	30.24	300–500	13	13	19	....
.45/90	300	1560	1285	1622	1100	2.17	10.65	28.43	300–500	13	13	....	....
.45/90 S. P. Smo.	300	1660	1361	1836	1234	1.90	9.30	25.15	300–500	....	15	....	....

AMMUNITION ENCYCLOPEDIA

Brief explanation of a few terms commonly used in connection with Ammunition and Fire Arms:

-A-

ACTION: The mechanism of a rifle, particularly the part that is employed in operating the rifle, i. e., loading and firing the rifle.

ALLOY: A mixture of metals. The term commonly used by riflemen to express the mixture of various metals with lead for bullets. The mixing of metals by fusing.

ANTIMONY: Used to alloy lead in bullets for hardening the projectile.

ANVIL: A small piece of metal, arrow-head in shape, which is placed inside the primer cup and which forms the point of resistance as the firing pin strikes the primer, thereby creating a friction which discharges the priming composition.

-B-

BALLING OF SHOT: Fusing of pellets caused by inferior wadding permitting powder gases to escape around the wads and thereby enter into the shot charge. Peters FELT wads embody the qualities which control the expanding powder gases resulting in maximum efficiency of the load.

BALLISTIC: The science of projection or projectiles.

BATTERY CUP: A small cup which contains the primer. In Peters shells the inner part of the cup is upset or spread out over the base wad which completely rivets all components of the head into a solid compact construction, all of which is gas tight and which makes it impossible for the base wad to be drawn out into the barrel of the gun due to suction caused by the travel of the load, (hence Peters "Rivet Battery Cup".)

BEVEL CRIMP: A type of crimp originated and perfected by Peters for shot gun shells which assures smooth working of the shell in all types of guns. Although used by others in some form or another, Peters crimp is still in a class by itself.

BLACKING THE SIGHT: To blacken the sight by painting or smoking. Gum camphor is commonly used for this purpose.

BORE: Synonymous to gauge. The diameter of the gun barrel.

BREECH: The rear extremity of the rifle.

BULGING: The swelling of a gun barrel caused by an obstruction in the barrel.

BULLET—*Cannelured Bullet*: An elongated bullet with grooves around the bullet. These grooves are for holding lubricant or for crimping purposes.

Elongated Bullet: Longer than it is wide, the opposite type from the round bullet.

Flat Pointed: Flat nosed. One with a flat nose.

Hollow Point Bullet: One with a hollow point for the purpose of increasing the mushrooming effect upon impact.

Metal Cased Bullet: One with a jacket of metal which completely encases the nose.

Metal Bullet Point: Bullet having lead bearing and metal tip.

Soft Point Bullet: A metal cased bullet with a tip of lead, so that on impact the bullet will mushroom, thereby increasing the striking energy.

Protected Point Expanding Bullet (**patented**): A type of Big Game bullet obtained only in Peters cartridges, which delivers maximum shocking power through a combination of perfect expansion or mushrooming and extreme penetration. (See page 17.)

BARREL TIME: Measured from the fall of the hammer to the muzzle of the gun.

-C-

CALIBER OF A RIFLE: A term synonymous to gauge (diameter of bore measured in one hundredths of an inch).

CHAMBER: The rear end of a barrel which receives the shell or cartridge.

CHILLED SHOT: Refers to hard shot. Hard shot is produced through mixing of antimony with the lead.

CHOKE: The decreased diameter of a shot gun barrel toward the muzzle. For the purpose of regulating the spread or pattern of the shot.

COMBUSTION: Burning of the powder in the barrel.

CONE: The reduction of diameter which in a barrel joins the chamber to the bore.

CORROSION: The deterioration on the inside of the barrel caused by the chemical action of the products of combustion after firing, usually caused by neglect.

CRIMP: Crimped—Crimping: A mechanical operation employed in loading metallic cartridges, which consists in turning over slightly or compressing the mouth of the metallic shell, or case, for the purpose of holding the bullet securely in its place. Applied also to shot shells. (See page 88, "Bevel Crimp".)

-D-

DROP: As applied to a gun stock—it means downward bend.

DROP SHOT: Soft shot.

-E-

ENERGY: The force or power of a charge.

EROSION: The actual wear on the inside of a barrel produced by the flame and gases of the ignited powder.

EXTRACTOR: The part of gun mechanism that withdraws the shell or cartridge from the chamber.

EJECTOR: Mechanism which throws the fired shell or cartridge from the arm.

-F-

FULMINATE: One of the ingredients of the priming mixture.

-G-

GALLERY LOAD: A light or reduced charge in cartridges for use indoors.

GAUGE: Diameter of the gun barrel. "12 Ga.", for instance, means that 12 round lead balls of this diameter weigh one pound; lead balls the size of a 10 ga. gun weigh ten to the pound; a 16 ga. gun, sixteen to the pound, etc.

GROOVES: The cavities inside a rifle barrel, which are usually spiral, and by which a bullet when expanded and forced forward receives a spinning motion giving to it an accurate flight.

-H-

HANGFIRE: Delayed or slow combustion.

-I-

IMPACT: A blow. A bullet striking an object.

-J-

JACKET: A covering for a bullet.

-K-

KEYHOLE: Refers to the shape of the bullet hole in the target resulting from the bullet traveling off its axis.

-L-

LANDS: A rifle barrel is bored to a desired size; the inside of the barrel is then called the surface; the grooves are cut from the surface. The raised spiral surfaces left by this operation are the lands.

LEADING: The term used to designate the presence of lead on the inside of a barrel.

-M-

MACHINE REST: An arrangement to which a rifle is affixed, or rested on to test for accuracy.

MID-RANGE: The distance between short range and long range.

MUSHROOMING: Upsetting or expanding of bullet on impact.

MUZZLE VELOCITY: The velocity of a bullet at the muzzle.

-O-

O'CLOCK: A term used by riflemen to indicate the location of a shot, or the direction from which the wind is blowing. To illustrate: Face the target with watch in hand and with the back of watch toward target. A shot in the line of figure XII would be a 12 o'clock shot; in the line of III, a 3 o'clock shot; in the line of VI, a six o'clock shot, etc.

-P-

PATTERN: Refers to the distribution of the shot charge after leaving the muzzle.

PERCENTAGE OF PATTERN: Number of pellet marks in a thirty inch circle, over a forty yard range, divided by the number of pellets in the load.

POWDER CHARGE: The amount of powder used in a load.

POWDERS: The powders used in loading are of three types: Black, Semi-Smokeless and Smokeless. Although black powder is still loaded by some companies, it has been antiquated by Semi-Smokeless—a remarkable powder, obtainable only in Peters ammunition. Semi-Smokeless is neither a smokeless nor a black powder nor a mixture of the two, but contains the admitted good qualities of both. Conspicuous among its merits may be mentioned these: high velocity with superior accuracy—absence of fouling—greatly lessened heat and less smoke than black powder. Smokeless powders are divided into two types. The first is known as Bulk, meaning its charge corresponds, or nearly so, in bulk to the charge of black powder; the second is the Dense type, which means a denser or much less in bulk.

PRIMER: A metallic cup charged with a priming composition; a blow from a hammer or plunger striking the primer ignites the powder charge.

-R-

RECOIL: The backward movement of a gun in the act of discharge.

REENTRY: Entering again; a term usually connected with reentry matches.

RICOCHET: RICOCHET SHOT: A glancing shot.

RIM-FIRE: A term applied to a cartridge fired by a blow on the rim of the head of a cartridge. Rim-fire rifle or pistol, one that fires a rim-fire cartridge.

RIVET BATTERY CUP: See Battery cup.

ROLLING A RIFLE: Rolling the rifle to one side or the other while aiming; not holding it plumb, the result of which is to send the shots in the direction in which the rifle is rolled. Same as canting a rifle.

-S-

SEMI-SMOKELESS POWDER: See Powders.

SHOCKING POWER: The force delivered by the projectile on impact; the result brought about through combination of striking energy and penetration.

SHOOT-OFF: A term generally used to mean the settlement of a tie by firing more shots to further test skill or decide supremacy.

SIGHTING SHOT: Shots fired to learn if the sights are correct, or learn the elevations, windage, or drift.

SPREADER LOAD: A Peters shot gun load which spreads its pattern over short ranges; used in bushy sections. (Peters Spreader Load, see page 104.)

SQUIB: SQUIB LOAD: A defective load. An extremely weak sounding load.

"STEEL WHERE STEEL BELONGS": A steel cup inside the brass cup which covers the entire head and rim of Peters H. V. and Target shells—added protection to the shooter which prevents bursted rims, blow-backs, gas leaks, etc.—an idea originated and developed by The Peters Cartridge Company.

STRIKING ENERGY: The force of the impact measured in foot pounds.

-T-

TACK-HOLE: The exact center of a bulls-eye—sometimes a small spot in the center of a bulls-eye, to which this term is also applied. Peters .22 Long Rifle "Tack-Hole" cartridges derive their name from this term because of their remarkable accuracy and uniformity. (See pages 14 and 20.)

TAKE DOWN SYSTEM: or TAKE DOWN RIFLE: An arm, the barrel of which can readily be taken from the action; employed for securing compactness in carrying the arm.

TRAJECTORY: As applied to bullets, the curve a bullet describes in its flight.

TRIGGER PULL: The amount of pressure necessary to release the trigger. Riflemen refer to this as a one-pound pull, or two pound pull, i. e., requiring a pressure of one or two pounds to release the trigger. A hair trigger pull; a very light pull; a creeping pull; a dragging pull; a still pull; a hard pull; a smooth pull; a fine pull, etc.

-U-

UNCRIMPED: Ammunition that is not crimped (See Crimp.)

-V-

VELOCITY: The speed of a projectile in its flight.

-W-

WAD: A yielding substance usually of felt, placed over the powder of a shot shell for the purpose of controlling gas blast. (See page 121.)

WINDAGE: The allowance made for drift of a bullet.

WOBBLE: A term applied to the unsteady rotation or spin of a bullet; usually caused by insufficient twist in the rifle barrel.

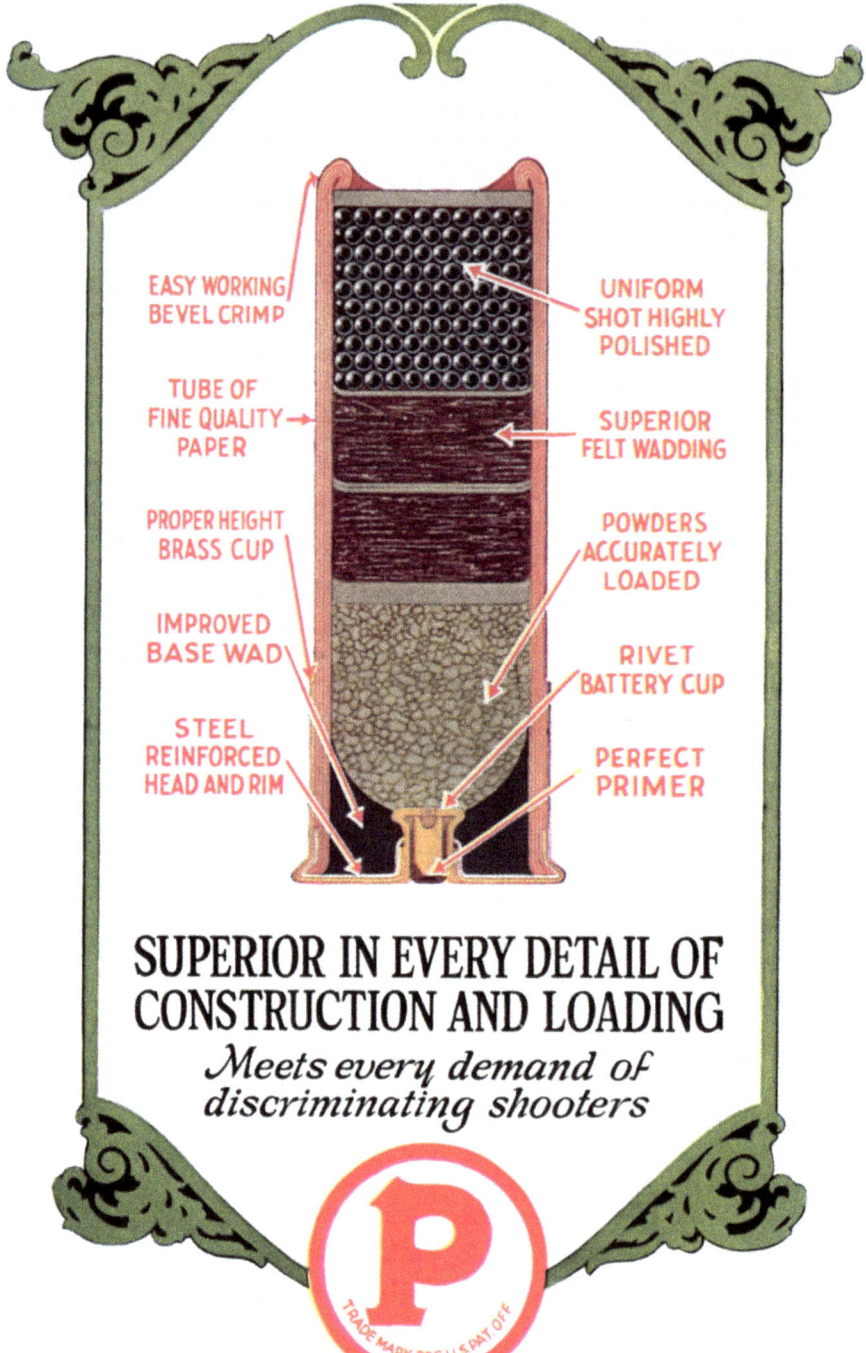

PETERS SHOT GUN SHELLS

The line of shotgun shells consists of four outstanding brands, namely, High Velocity, Target, Victor and Referee. The High Velocity shell is especially designed to give ballistic results beyond those obtained with the regular standard maximum load. The High Velocity shell has justly earned a national reputation among shooters as a superior long range shell because it is the only shell on the market especially designed for the use of progressive burning powder and this combined with Peters method of loading, develops the greatest efficiency of this type of powder. The Target shell is designed to handle the regular bulk or dense smokeless powders supplied in standard loads. For field or trap use the Target shell represents to the highest degree shot shell perfection.

Peters Victor shell was designed to meet the demand of shooters for a more popular priced smokeless shell and although low in price, the Victor is not only a Peters quality shell as regards materials, construction and load, but also has proved to be extremely effective in all shooting where the light and medium load combinations are sufficient.

The Referee shell meets in a really superior manner the existing demand for Black powder shells. The Referee is loaded with Semi-Smokeless powder which has proven to be superior to black powder in every way, but in spite of this fact, the Referee sells at the same price as black powder loads.

SHOT SHELL MANUFACTURING

Empty paper shot shells consist of the paper tube, base wad, steel reinforce ("stee where steel belongs"), brass head, battery cup and primer. The paper tube is made from paper especially manufactured for this purpose, under our direct supervision and in accordance with our own specifications, being rolled on machines designed and built by The Peters Cartridge Company.

The base wad is made from special paper manufactured under our own specifications. This "cushions" the blow of the explosion and in connection with the steel reinforcement, offers the necessary resistance to the powder gas at the base of the shell.

The steel reinforce ("steel where steel belongs") is used to reinforce the head of the shell, serving as additional protection where maximum loads are used, and is original with The Peters Cartridge Company.

In the "Heading" operation, the paper tube, brass cup and battery cup, base wad and steel reinforcement are assembled and headed to give the proper rim diameter and thickness and the proper compression and shape to the base wad. Likewise an important object of this operation is to so join the paper tube and brass head together that separation is impossible when the shell is used in the gun. By looking at a cross section of Peters shell head construction, it will be noted how the base wad and paper tube are forced into the rim formed by the brass cup and steel reinforcement and headed under great pressure, which holds the tube to the head and with the upsetting or rivetting of the battery cup, performed in this same operation, all components of the head are securely locked together, assuring against dislodged base wads, faulty extraction or tube separation.

The priming is done on special presses of unusual accuracy, and this operation completes the manufacture of the empty paper shells which are now sent to machines for loading, this to be fully described shortly.

*An operation in the making of Peters Famous Felt Wadding.
Showing a huge roll of felt being dried just previous to being cut up into sheets, pressed and lined. Felt of high quality has proven to be the most desirable wadding for shot shells, and careful examination will disclose that Peters felt wadding embodies these necessary qualities to a very superior degree—all because we make our felt in our own plant, and thus can insist upon and get felt of the desired quality.*

In the manufacture of elastic felt suitable for wadding in Peters shells, cattle hair of long, staple and special quality only is used. As in the case of all raw materials entering into the manufacture of Peters ammunition, the hair for this felt must measure up to Peters specifications, otherwise it will not be accepted for use.

The first operation in the manufacture of felt removes all foreign matter and dirt from the hair. The clean hair is then run through a machine which transforms it into filmy layers, several of which go to make up felt of the desired thickness.

The layers of hair are formed into rolls and then taken to the "Hardeners" where they are properly felted; they then pass through a machine and given a special treatment, developed by Peters, which greatly assists in giving the felt the quality of firmness and elasticity, so essential to good shot shell wadding. Operations too lengthy to describe here, requiring the greatest of care, are necessary in order to secure felt of an even thickness and density, all of which can be done correctly only by men of judgment and of long experience with Peters requirements. The felt is next cut into the desired length and pressed smooth preparatory to being lined on both sides with paper especially manufactured for this purpose. The lined sheets of felt are then subjected to a heat treatment and placed under pressure in automatic presses, it being extremely important in this operation that the proper pressure and timing of same be obtained in order to secure necessary results.

View in the boiler room of Peters huge power-house. Here steam is generated which provides the power and heat for the buildings and drying rooms of the Peters plant.

After passing through the cutting operation, the strips are passed to the wad-cutting machines. We now have a clean, elastic wad of even thickness, uniform size and density. In the next and last operation, the wads are passed through the greasing machines where a thin film of specially prepared lubricant is placed all around the edges, after which they are complete and ready for loading.

It will be noted that the felt wads made by the Peters method are entirely free from dirt and all foreign matter, and are of the proper elasticity and density, this being one of the main reasons for the superior ballistics obtained in all Peters loads.

The shot tower at the Peters plant is the latest and most modern structure of its kind in the country, and because of this fact Peters shot is of superior character, for in the building of this tower experiences of others were carefully analyzed, with the result that when completed it embodied the latest improvements and methods in the manufacture of shot.

The Peters shot tower is a concrete and brick structure of fourteen stories, and practically automatic from top to bottom. After the pig lead is heated to a molten state, the shot pellets are formed and dropped the full height of the tower into water to prevent mutilation. They are dried and run over a series of tables so designed and

Sorting Screens in Shot Tower—Here the round shot pellets are sorted as to size. This operation is extremely accurate in the results obtained—the reason why Peters shot of a given size are absolutely uniform.

operated as to remove all imperfect shot. Then each specific size is automatically separated, polished, and placed in the proper storage bin. The shot thus obtained are perfectly round, uniform in size and temper, highly polished and of superior quality.

Peters shells are loaded on automatic machines designed, perfected and used exclusively by Peters, which are almost human in their operations.

The powder charge is determined for any desired load and ingenious devices are provided on this machine to positively assure only correct loads passing through.

The ramming of the powder, wads and shot is performed by weighted rammers, insuring equal and uniform pressure on every load, this method being very much superior to that of a fixed rammer, which could not fail to give unequal pressures should there be any variations in the shot or in the thickness or density of the various wads. Peters shells have for years been loaded to uniform standards of velocity, pattern and penetration, and these are standards established by Peters. All bulk powders, irrespective of brand, are loaded to give the same ballistic results, load for load. All dense powders of equal specifications regardless of brand, are loaded not only to give relatively the same ballistics, but to give the same as the corresponding bulk powder load. This results in "Uniformity" to the highest degree.

The firm watertite, smooth-working, "bevel crimp" which is appreciated by all users of Peters shells, is the result of many years of study and development and is responsible for the perfect functioning of Peters shells in all kinds of arms and under all shooting conditions.

Scene in section of Ballistic Department—In this room Peters shells and cartridges are tested for functioning in the various arms and for casualties. Firearms of every make and description are found in a room adjacent, giving this department the facilities for subjecting the ⓟ Brand ammunition to the most practical and exhaustive tests.

The Ballistic Department is one of the most important in the plant, for it is here that goods in process and finished products are tested for the various qualities insisted upon by Peters. Instruments of the latest and most sensitive character keep a close check on all goods going through the plant, with the result that nothing is allowed to be shipped but what is as near perfect as is possible for man and science to make it.

Primers are tested by this Department for sensitiveness and ignition. All primers must fire within the limit of a pre-determined maximum blow, which has been decided as safely assuring the proper functioning of the primer in the gun. There is also a minimum blow determined, under which no primer should explode. This is to assure against over-sensitiveness.

The strength and heat of the primer flash and its adaptability to the various characters of powder, is determined by ignition tests. Ignition time is obtained by recording the time of the travel of the load from the fall of the hammer to the muzzle.

When the primers are approved for sensitiveness and ignition, they are then assembled in the shells. During this operation, the primed shells are being constantly tested by drop test and must fire within the limits of the maximum blows that have been determined.

INSPECTION TABLE—One of the many inspections which Peters Cartridges must pass before being approved for shipment.

Shot shells and cartridges are constantly selected at random from the different machines and taken to the Ballistic Department for testing; the shot shells are tested for functioning, velocities, pressures and patterns. Metallic cartridges are tested for functioning in the various rifles for velocity, pressure, energy and penetration. These tests are made constantly throughout the day. Thousands of shells and cartridges are fired and tested daily in the Ballistic Department, all for the purpose of maintaining an absolute Quality product.

We now have the completed product and one can see, to a certain extent, what a complicated yet interesting problem the manufacture of Small Arms ammunition is, especially where Quality is the first consideration. There is absolutely no guess work, every detail and every operation must be given the most careful attention by workmen of unusual experience. The Peters Inspection Force functions along the lines of an efficient Police Force—each member has his own particular "beat" to cover, he is entirely responsible for the character of goods which that "beat" produces. This Inspection Force knows Peters requirements and is held responsible for the quality of the product from the time the raw materials are received until the finished cartridges and shells are packed into the cases, ready for shipment. Peters standards are strictly maintained at all times, regardless of cost.

Such is the story of the manufacture of Peters "Quality Ammunition". It is plain to be seen nothing is left undone and no effort considered too great in our desire to place in the hands of discerning shooters loads that will not only produce superior results, which will do full justice to the users ability, but which are a credit to the manufacturer producing same.

THE PETERS CARTRIDGE COMPANY

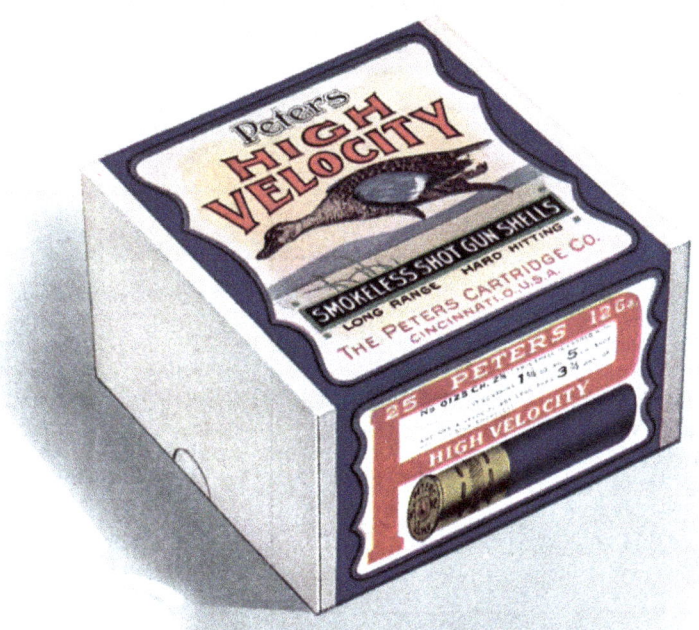
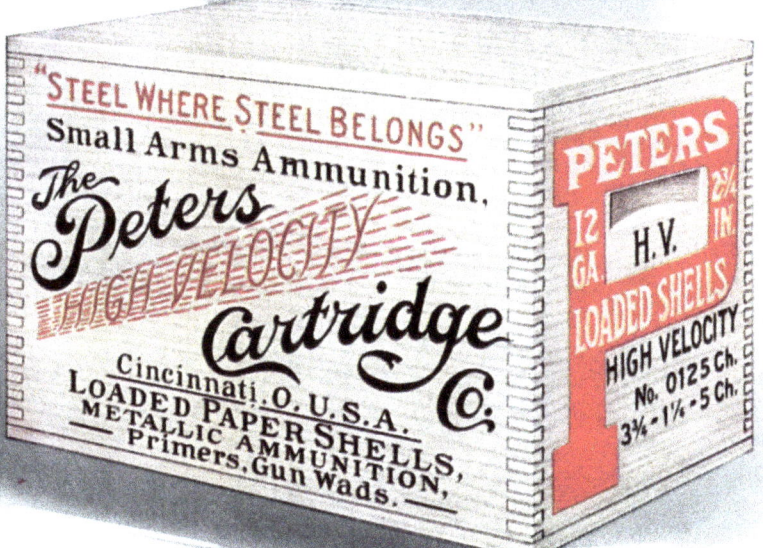

LOADED SHOT GUN SHELLS

"HIGH VELOCITY" (H. V.)

"steel where steel belongs"

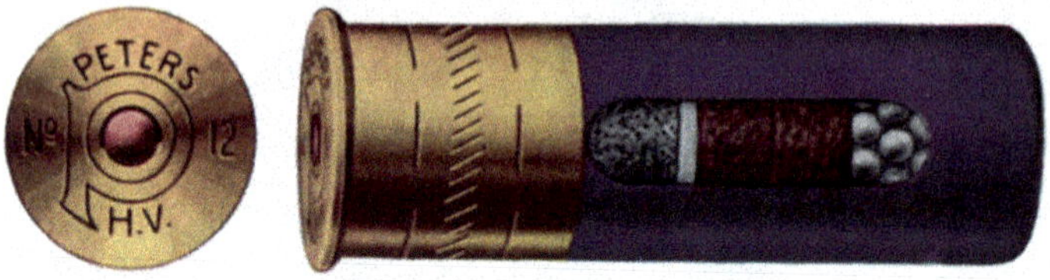

No. 3½ Primer

The "High Velocity" is the latest addition to the PETERS line. It is an *especially designed* shell for loads heavier than appear in regular standard list and is furnished only in the load combinations listed. It is what its name indicates—a high velocity, long range and hard hitting load. It is loaded with progressive burning smokeless powder, and is the only shell on the market especially designed and manufactured for extreme high velocity long range shooting. It should be used only in guns in good condition, intended for maximum loads.

10 GAUGE

Load No.	Length of Shell	Powder	Oz. Shot	Shot Sizes	List Price per 1,000	Telegraphic Cipher
0100.......	2⅞"	Equiv. 4¾ drs.	1⅝	2-3-4-5-6 Chilled	$68.50	Gadewing
010BB.....	2⅞"	Equiv. 4¾ drs.	1⅝	BB	68.50	Galleying

12 GAUGE

* 0120.....	2¾"	Equiv. 3¾ drs.	1¼	2-4-5-6-7-7½ Chilled	$56.50	Gauzying
* 012BB...	2¾"	Equiv. 3¾ drs.	1¼	BB	56.50	Galloping
**0130.....	3"	Equiv. 3¾ drs.	1⅜	2-4-5-6-7-7½ Chilled	68.50	Goviling
**013BB..	3"	Equiv. 3¾ drs.	1⅜	BB	68.50	Gophering

*Also supplied in 2⅞ in. and 3 in. lengths, in full case lots of 500, at a list price of $66.50 per 1,000.

**Supplied only in full case lots of 500.

16 GAUGE

0160.......	2 9/16"	Equiv. 3 drs.	1⅛	4-5-6-7-7½ Chilled	$53.50	Gevuting

Also supplied in 2¾ in., 2⅞ in. and 3 in. lengths, in full case lots of 500, at a list price of $63.50 per 1,000.

20 GAUGE

0200.......	2¾"	Equiv. 2¾ drs.	1	4-5-6-7-7½ Chilled	$51.75	Gilmaing

Also supplied in 2⅞ in. and 3 in. lengths, in full case lots of 500, at $61.75 per 1,000.

*** .410 CAL.**

0410.......	2½"	Equiv. ⅝ drs.	⅜	4-5-6-7½-8-9-10 Ch.	$33.25	Goating

**For 2 inch 410 shell see page 105.

In ordering, give load number, size of shot and specify "High Velocity."

The final figure of the load number indicates the size of shot and may be varied according to the size desired. Thus 0122 ch. means 12 ga., 2 ch.; 0127 ch., means 12 ga., 7 ch.

"In telegraphing, give cipher word, name of powder and size of shot."

LOADED SHOT GUN SHELLS

"TARGET"
(Reg. U. S. Pat. Off.)

"steel where steel belongs"

 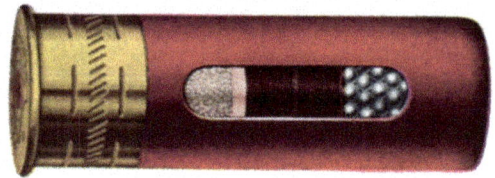

PETERS No. 3½ PRIMER

Bulk or Dense Smokeless Powders

The "Target" shell is the highest possible grade of smokeless shell supplied in standard load combinations, and will give the shooter the same one hundred per cent quality, as has been heretofore supplied in our "Ideal" and "Premier" shells. The "Target" was formerly loaded only with bulk smokeless powders, but is now supplied loaded with either bulk or dense smokeless, the shell being especially manufactured for the kind of powder with which it is loaded. It has all the Peters superior features, including "steel where steel belongs," rivet battery cup, watertite bevel crimp, uniform and superior waterproofing, elastic hair felt wadding, Peters uniform and perfectly finished shot, and Peters exclusive method of loading. The load is fully branded on the shell, label and case.

All standard brands of American bulk and dense smokeless powders are loaded in the "Target" shell.

The following letters prefixed to load numbers may be used to indicate kind of smokeless powder:

D for DuPont
S for Schultze
N for Ballistite

E for E. C.
DS for Dead Shot
L for Infallible

The final figure of the load number indicates the size of shot, and may be varied according to the size desired. Thus, No. 3104 means 2¾ drs. 1 oz. No. 4 shot; No. 3108, the same load with No. 8 shot; No. 3100, the same load with No. 10 shot, etc.

"TARGET" LOADED SHELLS

Bulk Powder in Drams—DuPont, E. C., Dead Shot and Schultze.
Dense Powders in Grains—Infallible and Ballistite.

10 GAUGE—2⅞ in.

Series No.	Powder Drs. Grs.	Ozs. Shot	Sizes Soft Shot	Soft Shot per M	Sizes Chilled Shot	Ch. Shot per M	Telegraphic Cipher
3330	3½ 28	1¼	4-6.............	$55.25	4-6.........	$58.25	Fervent
3370	4¼ 34	1¼	4-6.............	59.00	2-4-5-6......	62.00	Fever
337BB	4¼ 34	1¼	BB.............	62.00	....	.....	Ferro

+12 GAUGE

3100	2¾ 22	1	4-6-8-10........ *	$45.00	....	.....	Facade
°3120	2¾ 22	1⅛	6-8............ *	46.75	7½-8........	49.75	Fakir
3110	3 24	1	4-5-6-7-7½-8-9-10..*	46.25	4-6-7½......	49.25	Facet
°3140	3 24	1⅛	2-4-5-6-7-7½-8-9-10 *	48.00	4-5-6-7-7½-8-9	51.00	Fanatic
314BB	3 24	1⅛	BB............. *	51.00	....	.....	Fragrancy
3150	3 24	1¼	.... †	.....	7½..........	52.75	Fatigue
3180	3⅛ 25	1¼	.... †	.....	7½..........	54.00	Float
3160	3¼ 26	1⅛	2-4-5-6-7-7½-8.... *	49.25	2-4-5-6-7-7½-8	52.25	Fawn
316BB	3¼ 26	1⅛	BB............. *	52.25	....	.....	Fanfoot
3170	3¼ 26	1¼	4-5-6........... †	51.00	4-5-6-7½.....	54.00	Feign
317BB	3¼ 26	1¼	BB............. †	54.00	....	.....	Franchise
3220	3½ 28	1	4-5-6........... †	48.75	4-5-6........	51.75	Flustrate
3230	3½ 28	1⅛	2-4-5-6......... †	50.50	2-4-5-6-7½...	53.50	Famous
323BB	3½ 28	1⅛	BB............. †	53.50	....	.....	Farac
+3240	3½ 28	1¼	2-4-5-6......... †	52.25	2-4-5-6-7.....	55.25	Fang

+16 GAUGE—2 9/16 in.

3510	2½ 20	⅞	4-6-8...........	$43.25	4-6-7½.......	$46.25	Fight
3530	2½ 20	1	2-4-5-6-7-7½-8-9-10..	45.00	4-5-6-7-7½-8-9	48.00	Filter
353BB	2½ 20	1	BB.............	48.00	....	.....	Freakish
3520	2¾ 22	⅞	4-5-6-7-8........	44.50	4-5-6-7½.....	47.50	Filbert
3540	2¾ 22	1	5-6-7-7½-8.......	46.25	4-5-6-7-7½-8..	49.25	Fillet
♦3550	2¾ 22	1⅛	4-5-6...........	48.00	4-5-6-7½.....	51.00	Fiber
♦3560	3 24	1	....	.....	4-5-6-7½.....	50.50	Fizzle

+20 GAUGE—2½ in.

3710	2 16	¾	6-7½............	$41.50	6-7½.........	$44.50	Foment
3720	2¼ 18	¾	4-5-6-7-8........	42.75	4-5-6-7½.....	45.75	Frantic
3730	2¼ 18	⅞	2-4-5-6-7-7½-8-9-10..	44.50	4-5-6-7-7½-8-9	47.50	Fondle
373BB	2¼ 18	⅞	BB.............	47.50	....	.....	Freebooter
▲3750	2½ 20	⅞	.... †	.....	4-5-6-7½.....	48.75	Frigate
▲3740	2½ 20	1	6-7-7½-8........ †	47.50	4-5-6-7-7½...	50.50	Frad

*Loaded only in 2⅝ inch shells.
†Loaded only in 2¾ inch shells.
+Supplied in extra length shells in full case lots, at special list price (see basis, page 106.)
▲Also furnished in Oval powder loaded only in 2½ inch shells.
♦Supplied only in Oval powder when bulk powder is specified.
°7½ and 8 ch. shot furnished in 2¾ inch shell when so specified.
++Supplied also in Oval powder when specified.
"In telegraphing, give cipher word, name of powder, and size of shot. When chilled shot is wanted add "ing" to the cipher word.

"TARGET" SPREADER LOADS
12 GAUGE—2⅝ in.

Series No.	Powder Drs.	Powder Grs.	Ozs. Shot	Sizes Soft Shot	Soft Shot per M	Sizes Chilled Shot	Ch. Shot per M	Telegraphic Code
3140	3	24	1⅛	6-7½-8	$51.00	6-7½	$54.00	Fugue
16 GAUGE—2⁹⁄₁₆ in.								
3530	2½	20	1	6-8	$48.00	6-7½	$51.00	Funnel
20 GAUGE—2½ in.								
3730	2¼	18	⅞	6-8	$47.50	6-7½	$50.50	Fuss

In ordering Spreader loads always specify "Spreader."

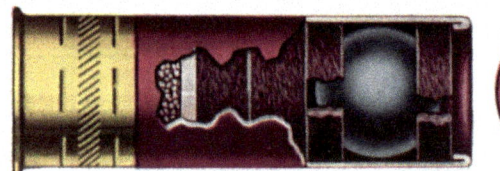

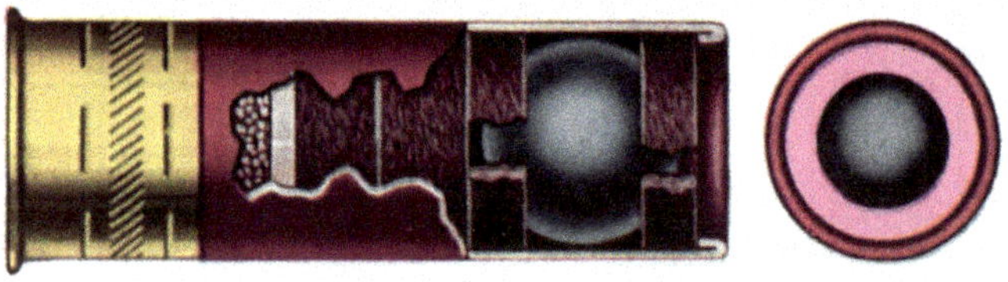

"TARGET" SINGLE BALL LOADS

Gauge No.	Powder Drs.	Powder Grs.	Weight of Ball	List per 1,000	Length of Shell	Telegraphic Code
12	3	24	1	$53.00	2⅝	Fountain
16	2½	20	⅞	50.00	2⁹⁄₁₆	Fossil
20	2	16	⅝	48.00	2½	Fortune

"TARGET" BUCK SHOT LOADS
12 GAUGE—2⅝ in.

Load No.	Powder Charge	Shot Charge	Size	Pellets in Layer	Layers	Pellets in Load	List Per 1,000	Telegraphic Code
X281	3¼ dr. or 26 gr.	1⅛ oz.	00	3	3	9	$52.25	Flaccid
X283	3¼ dr. or 26 gr.	1 oz.	1	4	3	12	51.00	Flambeau
X285	3¼ dr. or 26 gr.	1 oz.	3	†7	3	20	51.00	Flagon
*X287	3½ dr. or 28 gr.	1¼ oz.	0	3	4	12	55.75	Flash
16 GAUGE—2⁹⁄₁₆ in.								
X298	2½ dr. or 20 gr.	¾ oz.	1	3	3	9	$46.25	Florentine
20 GAUGE—2½ in.								
X304	2¼ dr. or 18 gr.	⅞ oz.	3	4	4	16	$47.50	Flexible

*Supplied in Oval powder only, when bulk powder is specified.
†6 in top layer.

Numbers heretofore used to indicate Eastern sizes have been adopted as standard and are shown in this list. When placing order for buck shot loads, these numbers should be used exclusively.

When telegraphing give cipher word and size of shot. When chilled shot is wanted add "ing" to cipher word.

28 GAUGE LOADED SHELLS

PETERS No. 3½ PRIMER

Loaded with Smokeless Powder

Load No.	Drs. Powder	Ozs. Shot	Size of Shot	List per 1,000 Ch.	Lgth. Shell inches	Telegraphic Cipher
28 Ga.	1¾	⅝	4-6-7½........	$50.50	2½	Futile

.410 PAPER SHOT SHELLS

(12 m/m.)   (36 Gauge)

PETERS No. 1½ PRIMER

Loaded with Smokeless Powder

Designed to meet a growing demand for a paper shot shell for shooting **pests and small animals and game birds**. The ideal ammunition for squirrels, rabbits, muskrats and small birds where the larger gauges are not only unnecessary, but too powerful.

These shells are adapted to all standard guns of .410 caliber including Stevens, Marble, H. & R. and others. They have an effective range of 25 to 35 yards and are of the same exceptional high quality as other goods bearing the Ⓟ brand.

Load No.	Drs. Powder	Ozs. Shot	Size of Shot	List per 1,000 Soft	List per 1,000 Ch.	Lgth. Shell inches	Telegraphic Cipher
†410 Ga.	5/6	3/10	4-5-6-7½-9........		$30.50	2	Further
*410 Ga.	5/6	1/5	Single Ball........	$37.00		2	Fusible

*No other single ball loads will be supplied.

For 2½ inch .410 load see High Velocity, page 100.

†In ordering be sure and specify length. Thus, .414, 2 in., indicates .410 shell No. 4 shot.

When telegraphing give cipher word and size of shot. When chilled shot is wanted add "ing" to cipher word.

"TARGET" SHELLS

Basis for Computing List Price of Special Loads

	Per 1,000
10 gauge, 3½ drams powder or equivalent, 1¼ ounce soft shot	$55.25
12 gauge, 2¾ drams powder or equivalent, 1 ounce soft shot	45.00
16 gauge, 2½ drams powder or equivalent, ⅞ ounce soft shot	43.25
20 gauge, 2 drams powder or equivalent, ¾ ounce soft shot	41.50
28 gauge, 1¾ drams powder, ⅝ ounce soft shot	47.50
.410 gauge, 5/6 drams powder, 3/10 ounce soft shot	27.50

For Target loads not listed on preceding pages, add to the above basis.

For each ¼ dram bulk smokeless or 2 grains dense smokeless	$ 1.25
For each ⅛ ounce shot	1.75
For Chilled shot add to the above basis	13.00
For Buck shot and lettered sizes add to above basis	13.00
For Dust shot add to the above basis	15.75
For Soft shot add to above basis	10.00

For special length shells.

12 gauge, 2⅞ in. or 3 in. lengths, add to above basis	10.00
16 gauge, 2¾ in., 2⅞ in., 3 in. lengths, add to above basis	10.00
20 gauge, 2⅞ in. or 3 in. lengths, add to above basis	10.00

Size 7½ shot furnished at regular list where shown. Where not shown it will be furnished as special load. No other half sizes supplied.

No deduction for powder or shot is made when either one is lighter than given in basis.

Regular Card-board and Black-edge wadding only will be furnished in "Target" shells.

Bulk Smokeless Powder loaded by dram measure only; no bulk powder loads marked in grains will be supplied.

Orders for loads not listed accepted only in case lots of 500.

MAXIMUM LOADS IN "TARGET" SHELLS

	Bulk Smokeless	Dense Smokeless	Shot
10 gauge	4¼ drs.	34 grs.	1¼ oz.
12 gauge	3½ drs.	28 grs.	1¼ oz.
16 gauge	3 drs.	24 grs.	1 oz.
†20 gauge	2½ drs.	20 grs.	1 oz.
28 gauge	1¾ drs.		⅝ oz.
.410 gauge	5/6 drs.		3/10 oz.

Note—The above prices apply **Only to Smokeless Powder** loads.

All Loaded Shells packed 25 in box; 500 in case.

†—Supplied in 2¾" shell also 2½" shell but loaded with Oval powder only.

LOADED SHOT GUN SHELLS
"VICTOR"
(Reg. U. S. Pat. Off.)

No. 3½ Primer
Loaded with Smokeless Powder

A smokeless shot shell, embodying the Peters high standard of quality in materials and loading. Supplied with Smokeless powder of American manufacture and loaded on the same identical machines as those used for loading our other shot shells, insuring uniformity both as to powder and shot charges, and also as to pressure exerted upon both powder and wads. The VICTOR is wadded with Peters high quality FELT wads. It has the inimitable Peters smooth working "watertite" bevel crimp and the same perfect shot as in Peters higher priced shells and is primed with Peters No. 3½ primer with the riveted battery cup construction. For the usual field and trapshooting the Victor shell is unsurpassed.

The final figure of the load number indicates the size of shot and may be varied according to the size desired. Thus No. 5106 means 12 ga., 2¾ drams, 1 oz. No. 6 shot No. 5108, the same load with No. 8 shot, etc.

12 GAUGE—2⅝ in.

Series No.	Drs. Pdr.	Ozs. Shot	Sizes Soft Shot	Price Soft Shot Per M	Sizes Chilled Shot	Price Ch. Shot Per M	Telegraphic Cipher
5100	2¾	1	6-8...........	$39.25	....	....	Vagol
†5120	2¾	1⅛	....	....	7½-8.........	$43.75	Vikin
5110	3	1	4-5-6-7-8-10....	40.00	4-6-7½.......	43.00	Valta
†5140	3	1⅛	4-5-6-7-8-10....	41.50	4-5-6-7½-8-9....	44.50	Vente
5160	3¼	1⅛	2-4-5-6-7-8....	42.25	4-5-6-7½.......	45.25	Virtu
516BB	3¼	1⅛	BB...........	45.25	....	....	Vinic
*5150	3	1¼	....	....	7½...........	46.00	Viola

16 GAUGE—2 9⁄16 in.

5510	2½	⅞	4-6-8........	$39.25	4-6-7½.......	$42.25	Vassa
5530	2½	1	4-5-6-7-8-10....	40.75	4-5-6-7½-9.....	43.75	Vaqua
5520	2¾	⅞	4-6-8........	40.00	4-6-7½.......	43.00	Villa

20 GAUGE—2½ in.

| 5720 | 2¼ | ¾ | 4-6-8........ | $37.00 | 4-6-7½....... | $40.00 | Vibro |
| 5730 | 2¼ | ⅞ | 4-5-6-7-8-10.... | 38.50 | 4-5-6-7½-9..... | 41.50 | Vigum |

*Furnished in 2¾ inch shell length only.
†7½ ch. and 8 ch. furnished in 2¾" length when so specified.
Note—Special loads will not be furnished in Victor shells.
In telegraphing give cipher word and size of shot. When chilled shot is wanted add "ing" to cipher word.

PETERS TRAP LOADS

TARGET   VICTOR

There is not a trapshooting tournament held that Peters shells are not very much in evidence not only as to number of users but also as to the results obtained, in the way of high scores. The superior quality construction and exclusive method of uniform loading assures trap loads that embody to a greater degree all of the important requisites of winning ammunition. Sure fire primer—fast and uniform velocities—evenly distributed patterns—absence of disturbing recoil, and last but not least—absolute dependability. Especially is this dependability desirable when the race is close, when one or two birds will win, when to win requires perfect co-ordination of shooter, gun and ammunition—that's when these superior Peters qualities make themselves manifest and fully appreciated.

The following letters prefixed to load numbers may be used to indicate kind of smokeless powder supplied in the Target shell.

   D for DuPont.   E   for E. C.
   S for Schultze.   DS for Dead Shot.
   N for Ballistite.   L   for Infallible.

The final figure of the load number indicates the size of shot and may be varied according to the size desired; thus, No. 3127½ ch. means 2¾ drs., 1⅛ oz. No. 7½ Chilled shot; No. 3128 ch. the same load with No. 8 Chilled shot.

TARGET

12 GAUGE

Series Number	Powder		Ounces Shot	Chilled Shot	List Per M	Telegraphic Cipher
	Drs.	Grs.				
†3120	2¾	22	1⅛	7½, 8	$49.75	Fakir
†3140	3	24	1⅛	7½, 8	51.00	Fanatic
*3150	3	24	1¼	7½	52.75	Fatigue
*3180	3⅛	25	1¼	7½	54.00	Float

VICTOR

Smokeless Powder

12 GAUGE

Series Number	Powder	Ounces Shot	Chilled Shot	List Per M	Telegraphic Cipher
	Drs.				
†5120	2¾	1⅛	7½, 8	$43.75	Vikin
†5140	3	1⅛	7½, 8	44.50	Vente
*5150	3	1¼	7½	46.00	Viola

*Furnished in 2¾ inch shell only.
†Furnished in 2⅝ inch and 2¾ inch shell.

MEMORANDA

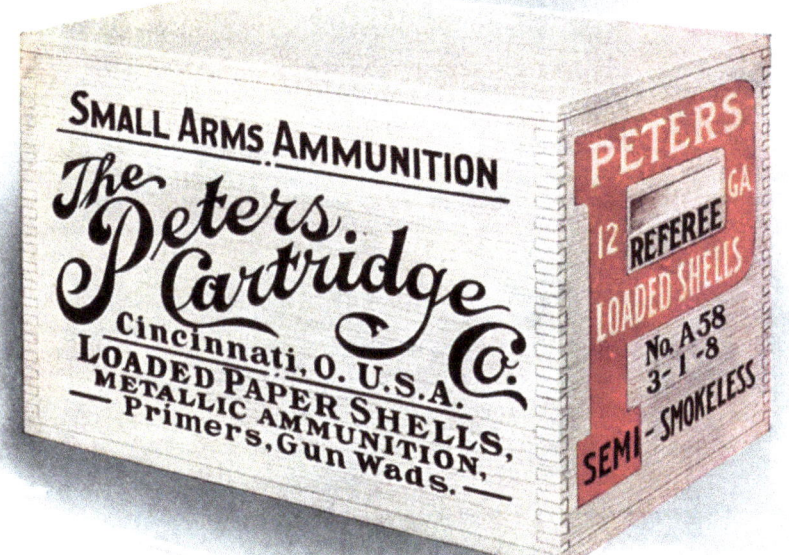

LOADED SHOT GUN SHELLS

"REFEREE"

(Reg. U. S. Pat. Off.)

No. 2 Primer

Loaded only with Semi-Smokeless Powder

This powder, with slight additional smoke, gives results equal to the best standard smokeless powder, yet the "Referee" is sold at the same price as black powder shells of other makes. Semi-Smokeless is manufactured under letters patent, and cannot be used by any ammunition manufacturer except The Peters Cartridge Company. The "Referee" therefore has no rival in the ammunition market. It has the velocity of the standard smokeless powders; at the same time it has the low breech pressure of black powder, and is as safe to shoot as black.

The "Referee" may be shot indefinitely without cleaning the gun or injuring the barrel. The powder is quick of ignition and absolutely reliable in all climates and under all conditions. It is pleasant to shoot, and is very superior in the field, where long, clean kills are desired.

The wadding is the finest quality of clean felt, manufactured by us for this purpose. It is free from dirt, prevents leading and is an important factor in securing standard velocity and excellent pattern.

Notwithstanding that the "Referee" is vastly superior to black powder shells and equal in many respects to smokeless loads, it is sold at the same price as black powder in other brands of shells.

The final figure of the load number indicates the size of shot, and may be varied according to the size desired. Thus, No. A94 means 3 drs. 1 oz. No. 4 shot; No. A98, the same load with No. 8 shot, etc.

"REFEREE" LOADED SHELLS

SEMI-SMOKELESS POWDER

10 GAUGE—2⅞ in.

Series No.	Drs. Pdr.	Ozs. Shot	Sizes Soft Shot	Soft Shot List Per M	Telegraphic Cipher
B70	4	1⅛	2-4-5-6	$43.00	Beautify

12 GAUGE—2⅝ in.

Series No.	Drs. Pdr.	Ozs. Shot	Sizes Soft Shot	Soft Shot List Per M	Telegraphic Cipher
A20	2¾	1	4-6-8	37.00	Achieve
A90	3	1	2-4-5-6-7-8	37.00	Azure
A70	3¼	1⅛	2-4-5-6	39.25	Arm
A7BB	3¼	1⅛	BB	42.25	Afflux

16 GAUGE—2⁹⁄₁₆ in.

Series No.	Drs. Pdr.	Ozs. Shot	Sizes Soft Shot	Soft Shot List Per M	Telegraphic Cipher
C20	2½	⅞	4-5-6	36.25	Calm
C70	2¾	1	2-4-5-6	38.50	Celestial

20 GAUGE—2½ in.

Series No.	Drs. Pdr.	Ozs. Shot	Sizes Soft Shot	Soft Shot List Per M	Telegraphic Cipher
C220	2¼	¾	4-6	36.25	Culvert
C240	2½	⅞	4-6	36.25	Cuirass
C24BB	2½	⅞	BB	39.25	Culpable

28 GAUGE—2½ in.

Series No.	Drs. Pdr.	Ozs. Shot	Sizes Soft Shot	Soft Shot List Per M	Telegraphic Cipher
C270	1¾	⅝	4-6	33.50	Cumulate

We have discontinued listing the "LEAGUE" shell, loaded with black powder, but will furnish same when specified, in same combinations and at the same price as the "REFEREE" shell.

"In telegraphing, give cipher word, name of powder and size of shot."

"REFEREE" SHELLS

Basis for Computing List Price of Special Loads

SEMI-SMOKELESS

	Per 1,000
10 gauge, 4 drams, 1⅛ oz. soft shot	$43.00
12 gauge, 3 drams, 1 oz. soft shot	37.00
16 gauge, 2½ drams, ⅞ oz. soft shot	36.25
20 gauge, 2½ drams, ⅞ oz. soft shot	36.25
28 gauge, 1¾ drams, ⅝ oz. soft shot	33.50

For "Referee" loads not listed on preceding pages, add to the above basis:

For each ¼ dram of powder	$ 0.75
For each ⅛ oz. of shot	1.50
For Chilled Shot add to the above basis	13.00
For Buck Shot and lettered sizes add to above basis	13.00
For Dust Shot add to the above basis	15.75
For Soft Shot add to the above basis	10.00

No deduction for powder or shot is made when either one is lighter than given in basis.

Loads not shown in regular list will be supplied only on the above basis.

Orders for loads not listed accepted only in case lots of 500.

MAXIMUM SEMI-SMOKELESS LOADS

	Powder	Shot
*10 gauge	5 drs.	1¼ oz.
*12 gauge	3¾ drs.	1⅛ oz.
*16 gauge	3 drs.	1 oz.
20 gauge	2¼ drs.	⅞ oz.
28 gauge	1¾ drs.	⅝ oz.

*Not on regular list, see above basis for computing list price.

Note—The above basis applies to Semi-Smokeless only.

All Loaded shells packed 25 in a box; 500 in case.

YACHT GUN SHELLS
Loaded with Black Powder only.

Per M.

10 gauge 8 drams Black Powder $41.50
    Packed 25 in box; 500 in case.

LENGTHS OF LOADED SHELLS

For the purpose of securing uniformity in loading and maintaining a high standard of shooting qualities in our shells, we have adopted the following schedule of shell lengths for regular loads:

"REFEREE"

10 gauge	2 7/8 inch
12 "	2 5/8 "
16 "	2 9/16 "
20 "	2 1/2 "
28 "	2 1/2 "

"VICTOR"

12 gauge	2 5/8 - 2 3/4 inch
16 "	2 9/16 "
20 "	2 1/2 "

"TARGET"

10 gauge	2 7/8 inch
12 "	2 5/8 - 2 3/4 "
16 "	2 9/16 "
20 "	2 1/2 - 2 3/4 "

"HIGH VELOCITY"

10 gauge	2 7/8 inch
12 "	2 3/4 "
16 "	2 9/16 "
20 "	2 3/4 "
.410 "	2 1/2 "

"SMALL BORE SHELLS"

28 gauge	2 1/2 inch
.410 "	2 "

    For price of Shells in lengths not shown in regular list, see "Basis for computing list price of special loads."

EMPTY PAPER SHOT SHELLS

BLACK POWDER
Tan Color.
Using No. 2 Primer. For Black Powder.

				Telegraphic Code	List per M.
10 gauge	2⅞	inches		Devix	$16.25
10	"	3	"	Deter	17.25
12	"	2⅝	"	Demco	14.50
12	"	2¾	"	Demda	16.25
16	"	2 9/16	"	Deyer	14.25
20	"	2½	"	Diban	14.25
28	"	2½	"	Didra	17.25

SMOKELESS
"Steel Where Steel Belongs"

A beautiful dark red shell with high brass and Peters No. 3½ Primer, which gives instantaneous ignition to any standard Smokeless powder.

			Telegraphic Code	List per M.
10 gauge	2⅞	inches	Dirod	$21.00
12	"	2⅝ inches	Digli	19.00
12	"	2¾ inches	Digmo	21.00
12	"	2⅞ inches	Dilca	21.00
12	"	3 inches	D'nud	21.00
16	"	2 9/16 inches	Divun	18.00
16	"	2¾ inches	Dizaf	21.00
16	"	2⅞ inches	Dobov	21.00
16	"	3 inches	Dobpi	21.00
20	"	2½ inches	Doena	18.00
20	"	2¾ inches	Dohem	21.00
20	"	2⅞ inches	Dohga	21.00
20	"	3 inches	Dokaz	21.00

Will ship shells constructed for bulk Smokeless powder on orders when dense Smokeless shells are not specified.

SMALL BORE SHELLS
For use with bulk Smokeless powder.

	Telegraphic Code	List per M.
28 gauge 2½ in.—No. 3½ Primer	Domto	$18.00
.410 gauge (12mm.) 2 in.—No. 1½ Primer	Domud	15.25
.410 gauge (12 mm.) 2½ in.—No. 1½ Primer	Doily	17.00

All Empty Shells packed 100 in a box; 5,000 in case.

EQUIVALENT STRENGTH OF BLACK, SEMI-SMOKELESS, AND SMOKELESS POWDERS

Black Powder	King's Semi-Smokeless	Bulk Smokeless	Dense Smokeless	
			Infallible	Ballistite
Drams	Drams	Drams	Grains	Grains
2	2	2	16	16
2¼	2¼	2¼	18	18
2½	2½	2½	20	20
2¾	2¾	2¾	22	22
3	3	3	24	24
3¼	3¼	3¼	26	26
3½	3½	3½	28	28
3¾	3¾	3¾	30	30
4	4	4	32	32
4¼	4¼	4¼	34	34
4½	4½	4½	36	36

The prices appearing in this catalogue are list prices, and this list is subject to change without notice. Dealers furnish Peters Ammunition at regular retail prices. For further information address The Peters Cartridge Company, Cincinnati, Ohio, U. S. A.

PETERS COMPARATIVE SIZES OF SHOT

No.	Chilled Shot No. in Oz.	Drop Shot No. in Oz.	Diam. in Inches	Diam. in Millimeters
Dust	......	4565	.04	1.02
12	2385	2326	.05	1.27
11	1380	1346	.06	1.52
10	868	848	.07	1.78
9	585	568	.08	2.03
8	409	399	.09	2.28
7½	345	338	.09½	2.41
7	299	291	.10	2.54
6	223	218	.11	2.79
5	172	168	.12	3.02
4	136	132	.13	3.30
3	109	106	.14	3.53
2	88	86	.15	3.78
1	73	71	.16	4.06

Packed in 5-lb. and 25-lb. bags.

Prices quoted on application.

Numbers heretofore used to indicate Eastern sizes have been adopted as standard, and are so shown in this list. When placing orders for buckshot, these numbers should be used exclusively.

PETERS
COMPARATIVE SIZES OF BUCKSHOT

No.	Drop Shot No. in Oz.	Diameter in Inches	Diameter in Millimeters
B	59	.17	4.32
Air Rifle	56	.17 ½	4.44
BB	50	.18	4.57
BBB	42	.19	4.83
T	36	.20	5.08
TT	31	.21	5.33
F	27	.22	5.59

Size	Diameter in Inches	Diameter in Millimeters	Balls in Lb. (approx.)
4	.24	6.09	344
3	.25	6.35	299
2	.27	6.86	238
1	.30	7.62	175
0	.32	8.13	142
00	.34	8.64	118
000	.36	9.14	100

Packed in 5-lb. and 25-lb. bags.
Prices quoted on application.

Numbers heretofore used to indicate Eastern sizes have been adopted as standard, and are so shown in this list. When placing orders for buckshot, these numbers should be used exclusively.

LEAD BALLS

		Diameter in Inches	Diameter in Millimeters	Balls in Lb. (about)
	.410 Gauge	.380	9.65	85
	.44 Game Getter	.428	10.79	58.8
	28 Gauge	.511	12.95	35.5
	.20 Gauge	.545	13.84	29
	16 Gauge	.620	15.49	19.5
	12 Gauge	.650	16.38	17
	10 Gauge	.700	18.03	13.75

Prices quoted on application.

PETERS SPECIAL AIR RIFLE SHOT
Actual Size.

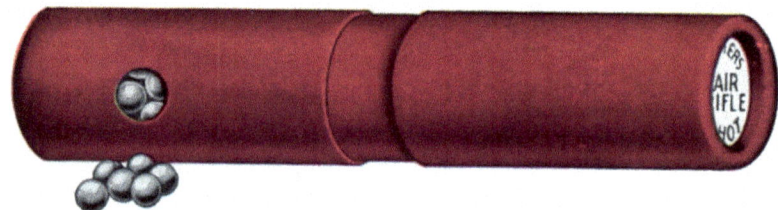

    In tubes for pocket use. By extending tube, shot can be removed as desired, or poured into barrel.
    100 tubes to a case. Gross weight, 30 lbs. Net weight, 25 lbs.
    Loose Air Rifle Shot also supplied in 1-lb., 5-lb. and 25-lb. bags.
    Prices quoted the trade on application.

GUN WADS

Cut from Best Elastic Felt, Made in Our Own Factories
(Unequaled for Density and Even Thickness.)

The Peters Cartridge Company makes its own felt, for gun wads only, using for this purpose specially selected, washed brown cattle hair and other high grade materials. In a shotgun shell the shot pattern, velocity, freedom from leading and from excessive recoil, all depend in a large measure upon the wadding. Because this is so vital a feature, The Peters Cartridge Company has for years made its own wads, so as to be able to control their quality. Peters wads contain no dirt or foreign material which would injure the barrel of the gun or in any other way be detrimental. Peters wads are so firmly knit together that they will not blow to pieces; they are very elastic, and will contract evenly at the choked muzzle of the gun. Peters wads, because of their perfect confinement of the gases and perfect lubrication, result in a finer shooting shell than is possible with any other make of wad.

BLACK EDGE

	3-16 inch Thick. Packed 250 in Box Per M.	¼ inch Thick. Packed 250 in Box Per M.	⅜ inch Thick. Packed 125 in Box Per M.
10 gauge.....	$2.70	$3.80	$6.30
12, 16, 20, 28, 410 gauge	2.25	3.25	5.85

VICTOR WADS

When Black Edge Wads without lubricant are wanted, they should be ordered by the name "Victor", as heretofore, at the same price as regular Black Edge Wads.

⅜ inch Black Edge and Victor wads are packed 10,000 in a case. All others 50,000 in case. 3-16 inch is standard and will be shipped unless otherwise specified.

CARDBOARD WADS

Cut from card board made especially for this purpose, of even thickness and density.

	"AA" Thickness over powder Heavy Per M.	"A" Thickness over powder Medium Per M.	"B" Thickness over shot Thin Per M.
10 gauge	$1.10	$1.10	$1.10
12, 16, 20, 28 gauge	1.05	1.05	1.05
410 gauge		1.05	1.05

All card board wads packed 50,000 to a case. "A" thickness will be shipped when orders do not specify otherwise.

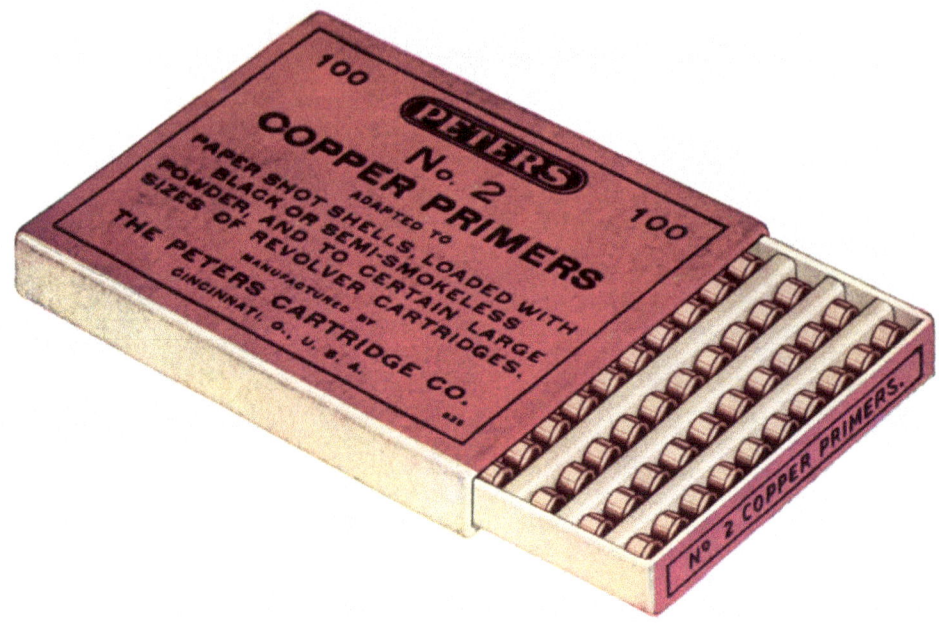

PETERS PRIMERS

Peters Primers are designed especially for the particular shell or cartridge for which they are intended, and are properly adapted to Semi-Smokeless and the different kinds of Smokeless powders with which they are to be used. They are absolutely sure-fire, with a hot, powerful flash, which results in quick, uniform ignition of the powder charge.

	Per M.	Telegraph Cipher
No. 1. Copper. For use in Revolver Cartridges, with Black, Semi-Smokeless or Smokeless powder.		
Packed 250 in box	$3.60	Keel
Packed 100 in box	3.80	Kennel
No. 1½. Copper. For Revolver Cartridges, with Black, Semi-Smokeless or Smokeless powder.		
Packed 250 in box	3.60	Kilt
Packed 100 in box	3.80	Kid
No. 2. Copper. For PETERS "Referee" and "League" Shot Shells.		
Packed 250 in box	3.60	Kick
Packed 100 in box	3.80	Kite
No. 2X. For Revolver Cartridges, with Black, Semi-Black, Semi-Smokeless or Smokeless powder.		
Packed 100 in box	3.80	Kyle
No. 3½. Used in PETERS "Victor," "Target," and "High Velocity" Shot Shells.		
Packed 100 in box	5.50	Kyntor
No. 6½. Brass. For Smokeless Rifle Cartridges.		
Packed 100 in box	3.80	Kutter
No. 11. Special Peters Primer. For High Power Cartridges.		
Packed 100 in box	3.80	Knit
No. 11½. Special Peters Primer. For High Power Cartridges.		
Packed 100 in box	3.80	Kelp

No. 3½ Primers packed 50,000 in a case; all others 100,000 in a case.

POPULAR LOADS FOR DIFFERENT SHOOTING

The loads suggested below were arrived at through popular demand. We do not mean to imply that any one of these combinations is the only load one can use for the game listed and get good results for there are no doubt other combinations which would prove just as effective, but for the purpose of giving those who may desire such information we list load combinations for various game shooting as determined from actual demand.

Character of Shooting	Shell	Gauge	POWDER			SHOT	
			Bulk Drs.	Dense Grs.	Semi-Smo. Drs.	Ozs.	Size
Trapshooting	Target	12	2¾	22		1⅛	7½*-8*
		12	3	24		1⅛	7½*-8*
		12	3	24		1¼	7½*
	Victor	12	3			1⅛	7½*-8*
		12	3			1¼	7½*
		12	2¾			1⅛	7½*-8*
Duck Brant Jack Rabbit	High Velocity	12	(a) see below			1¼	4*-5*-6*
		16	(a) see below			1⅛	4*-5*-6*
		20	(a) see below			1	4*-5*-6*
	Target	12	3½ or 3¼	28-26		1¼-1⅛	4-5-6
		16	3	24		1	4*-5*-6*
		20	2½	20		1	4*-5*-6
	Victor	12	3¼			1⅛	4-5-6
	Referee	12			3¼	1⅛	4-5-6
Duck Pheasant Grouse Prairie Chicken Partridge Hawk Crow	High Velocity	12	(a) see below				6*
		16	(a) see below				6*
		20	(a) see below				6*
	Target	12	3¼	26		1⅛	6
		16	2¾	22		1	6
		20	2½	20		1	6
	Victor	12	3¼			1⅛	6
		16	2¾			⅞	6
	Referee	12			3¼	1⅛	6
		16			2¾	1	6
Goose Turkey Fox Raccoon	High Velocity	12	(a) see below			1¼	BB-2*
		16	(a) see below			1⅛	4*
		20	(a) see below			1	4*
	Target	12	3½-3¼	28-26		1¼-1⅛	2*-BB
		16	3	24		1	4*
		20	2½	20		1	4*
	Victor	12	3¼			1⅛	2-BB

*Listed in Chilled Shot only.

(a) High Velocity shell is loaded to give a velocity in 12 ga. equivalent to 3¾ drs. of regular bulk smokeless powder; in 16 ga. equivalent to 3 drs.; 20 ga. equivalent to 2¾ drs. Where extreme long range—hard hitting results are desired the "High Velocity" shell has no equal.

POPULAR LOADS FOR DIFFERENT SHOOTING
(Continued)

Character of Shooting	Shell	Gauge	POWDER			SHOT	
			Bulk Drs.	Dense Grs.	Semi-Smo. Drs.	Ozs.	Size
Rabbit Squirrel	High Velocity	20	(a) see below			1	6*
	Target	12	3	24		1-1⅛	6-7
		16	2½-2¾	20-22		1	6-7
		20	2¼	18		¾	6-7
	Victor	12	3			1-1⅛	6-7
		16	2½			1	6-7
		20	2¼			⅞	6-7
	Referee	12			3	1	6-7
		16			2½	⅞	6
		20			2¼	¾	6
Snipe Rail Plover	Target	12	3	24		1⅛	8-9
		16	2½	20		1	8-9
		20	2¼	18		⅞	8-9
	Victor	12	3			1⅛	8-9*
		16	2½			1	8-9*
		20	2¼			⅞	8-9*
Quail Dove Woodcock	High Velocity	20	(a) see below			1	7½*
	Target	12	3	24		1⅛	7½-8
		16	2½	20		1	7½-8
		20	2¼	18		⅞	7½-8
	Victor	12	3			1⅛	7½*
		16	2½-2¾			1-⅞	7½*
		20	2¼			⅞-¾	7½*
	Referee	12			3	1	7-8
Wolf-Deer Black Bear Riot Duty Guard Duty	Target	12	3½	28		1¼	0-Buck Shot

*Listed in Chilled Shot only.

(a) High Velocity shell is loaded to give a velocity in 12 ga. equivalent to 3¾ drs. of regular bulk smokeless powder; in 16 ga. equivalent to 3 drs.; 20 ga. equivalent to 2¾ drs. Where extreme long range—hard hitting results are desired the "High Velocity" shell has no equal.

INDEX

	PAGE
Addenda	126
Air Rifle Shot	120
Ballistic Department	11, 97
Ballistic Table Popular Peters Cartridges	82-87
Basis for computing prices of Special loads, Referee Shells	114
Basis for computing prices of Special loads, Target Shells	106
Blank Cartridges	54-58
Brief History of The Peters Cartridge Company	5
Buck Shot	119
Buck Shot Loads	104
Center Fire Cartridges	25-53
Chemical Laboratory	8
Condensed Price List, Metallic Cartridges	64-80
Empty Paper Shot Shells	116
Encyclopedia of Ammunition—Terms commonly used	88-91
Equivalent Strength of Various Powders	117
Felt Wads	94, 95, 121
Four Ten Caliber Shot Shells	105
Gun Wads	94, 95, 121
High Velocity Cartridges	15, 16, 30, 36, 38, 42, 43, 44, 51
High Velocity Shot Shells	99, 100
Hollow Point Expanding Cartridges	16
Interchangeable Cartridges—Table of	81
Lead Balls	120
Lengths of Loaded Shells	115
Loaded Shells	93-115
Manufacturing Operations—	
Metallic Cartridges	9-11
Shotgun Shells	93, 98
Materials Used in the Manufacture of Peters Ammunition	7
Maximum Loads in Target Shells	106
Maximum Semi-Smokeless Loads (Referee Shells)	114
Memoranda	110
Metallic Cartridges (Illustrations and General Description)—	
Rim Fire	18-24
Center Fire Pistol, Revolver and Rifle	14, 25-40
Center Fire Military and Sporting	41-53
Popular Loads for different shooting	123, 124
Powders Loaded in Peters Metallic Cartridges	12
Primers	122
Protected Point Expanding Bullet	17, 42, 43, 44, 45
Quality Ammunition	5
Referee Shot Shells	111-114
Rice Leaders of the World Association Emblem	3
Rim Fire Cartridges	13, 18
Semi-Smokeless Powder	12, 112
Shooting Gallery Ammunition	13, 18
Shot Cartridges	59-63
Shot Gun Shells (General Description and Illustrations of Manufacturing Operations	93-98
Shot Sizes and Illustrations	118, 119
Single Ball Loads	104
Spreader Loads	104
Tack Hole Cartridges	14, 20
Target Shot Shells	101-106
Trap Loads	109
Twenty-eight gauge loaded shells	105
Twenty-two Short Cartridges	13-18
Victor Shot Shells	107, 108
Wads	94, 95, 121
Works of The Peters Cartridge Company	6, 7
Yacht Gun Shells	115

ADDENDA

All loads listed in this catalog are subject to change.

For domestic trade we adhere to the standard list of loads as recommended by the Division of Simplified Practice, Department of Commerce. For export trade see Export List.

Since this catalog went to press we have added buck shot and single ball loads to the High Velocity shell. For specific data see latest price list booklet.

THE
PETERS CARTRIDGE
COMPANY

ADDITIONAL CHANGES SINCE THIS BOOK WENT TO PRESS

.300 Cal. Savage Cartridge with 180 grain metal cased Hollow Point Expanding bullet has been added—list price $92.00 per 1000.

High Velocity shells will be furnished in either DuPont "Oval" powder or Hercules "Herco" powder.

Schultze and Ballistite powders have been discontinued by the manufacturer. We will furnish subject to stock on hand.

12 gauge Target shells, except Buckshot, Spreader, and Single Ball loads, will be supplied in any standard brand of American smokeless powder and will be so marked. 10, 16, 20, 28 and .410 gauge Target shells, and 12 gauge Target, Buckshot, Spreader, and Single Ball loads will be supplied with standard brands of American smokeless powder, unmarked, the particular brands loaded to be at our option.

List prices of .22 Short smokeless, .22 Long smokeless, .22 Long Rifle smokeless, in both hollow point and solid ball, are reduced to the list price of the same cartridges supplied with Semi-Smokeless powder.

Several metallic cartridges have been discontinued. See latest price list booklet.

THE PETERS CARTRIDGE COMPANY

www.ingramcontent.com/pod-product-compliance
Ingram Content Group UK Ltd.
Pitfield, Milton Keynes, MK11 3LW, UK
UKHW051351180426
11947UKWH00014B/875